Paleo Instant Pot

Paleo Diet Cookbook for Beginners with Delicious Paleo Instant Pot Recipes

Paleo Instant Pot Cooking
Book 5

By Brendan Fawn

Copyright © 2020 Brendan Fawn

All rights reserved.

ISBN: 9798696054650

Text Copyright © [Brendan Fawn]
All rights reserved. No part of this guide may be reproduced in any form without permission in writing from the publisher except in the case of brief quotations embodied in critical articles or reviews.

Legal & Disclaimer
The information contained in this book and its contents is not designed to replace or take the place of any form of medical or professional advice; and is not meant to replace the need for independent medical, financial, legal or other professional advice or services, as may be required. The content and information in this book has been provided for educational and entertainment purposes only.

The content and information contained in this book has been compiled from sources deemed reliable, and it is accurate to the best of the Author's knowledge, information, and belief. However, the Author cannot guarantee its accuracy and validity and cannot be held liable for any errors and/or omissions. Further, changes are periodically made to this book as and when needed. Where appropriate and/or necessary, you must consult a professional (including but not limited to your doctor, attorney, financial advisor or such other professional advisor) before using any of the suggested remedies, techniques, or information in this book.

Upon using the contents and information contained in this book, you agree to hold harmless the Author from and against any damages, costs, and expenses, including any legal fees potentially resulting from the application of any of the information provided by this book. This disclaimer applies to any loss, damages or injury caused by the use and application, whether directly or indirectly, of any advice or information presented, whether for breach of contract, tort, negligence, personal injury, criminal intent, or under any other cause of action.

You agree to accept all risks of using the information presented in this book.

You agree that by continuing to read this book, where appropriate and/or necessary, you shall consult a professional (including but not limited to your doctor, attorney, or financial advisor or such other advisor as needed) before using any of the suggested remedies, techniques, or information in this book.

Introduction to Paleo Diet 8

What to Eat and What Not? Consumable and Non - Consumable Food 8

Paleo Diet Nutrition 8

A Sample Paleo Menu for One Day 9

Instant Pot 11

About the Instant Pot 11

How to Use the Instant Pot Buttons 13

Instant Pot Paleo Beef Recipes 17

Paleo Beef Goulash with Tomato Sauce 17

Instant Pot Paleo Beef Ribs in BBQ Sauce 19

Paleo Beef Liver 21

Paleo Beef Meatballs with Carrots 23

Paleo Beef Liver with Onions 25

Veal with Mushrooms 26

Paleo Beef Chops with Onions and Brussels 27

Spicy Smoked Beef Clod 28

Spicy Paleo Beef Ribs in Sauce with Arugula 29

Bistecca alla Fiorentina Paleo Steak 31

Paleo Beef Stew 32

Paleo Beef Roulades with Dried Apricots 34

Smoked Paleo Instant Beef Roast 36

Instant Pot Paleo Pork Recipes 38

Paleo Pork Goulash 38

Paleo Pork Stew 40

Pork with BBQ Sauce and Cashews 42

Pork Chops with Ranch Dressing 43

Paleo Spare Ribs in BBQ Sauce 44

Pork Bouillon with Celery 45

Paleo Pork Rolls with Prunes and Raisins 46

Paleo Pork Rolls with Prunes and Pineapples 48

Paleo Instant Pork with Peanuts 49

Paleo Spicy Pork Ribs with Bell Peppers 51

Napa Cabbage with Sausages and Carrots 53

Spicy Pork Ribs with Mango 55

Jamaican Jerk Pork Roast 57

Pork Ribs with Celery in Honey 58

Paleo Pork Roulades with Apricots 60

Bacon and Pancetta in Lime Juice 62

Paleo Pork Rinds 63

Instant Pot Paleo Chicken, Turkey and Goose Recipes 64

Paleo Chicken Breast with Cheese 64

Paleo Chicken Rolls with Carrots 66

Paleo Goose with Pumpkin 68

Paleo Goose with Apples, Prunes and Apricots 70

Paleo Salsa Chicken 72

Paleo Turkey Steaks 74

Paleo Goose Curry with Broccoli 76

Paleo Keema Chicken with Zucchini 78

Paleo Chicken Wings with Walnuts 80

Turkey with Pumpkin Puree and Tomatoes 82

Baked Paleo Chicken Drumsticks 83

Paleo Turkey Roulades with Prunes and Raisins 85

French Goose with Oranges and Peanuts 86

Instant Goose in Spices 87

Turkey Chunks with Walnuts 88

Paleo Chicken with Pineapples and Apples 89

Paleo Turkey with Squash 90

Paleo Chicken with Apples 91

Paleo Chicken Thighs with Basil 93

Chicken Meatballs with Champignons 94

Paleo Chicken with Prunes 95

Zucchini Spaghetti with Chicken 96

Goose with Pumpkin Puree 97

Chicken Wings in Sauce 99

Chicken with Pumpkin and Tomatoes 100

Spicy Paleo Chicken Hearts Bouillon 102

French Chicken Livers with Tomatoes 103

Chicken Breast with Pineapple Rings 105

Paleo Creamy Chicken Soup 106

Chicken Breast with Zucchini 108

Paleo Soup with Chicken Sausages 110

Paleo Chicken Meatballs 111

Turkey with Pumpkin with Champignons 113

Paleo Chicken and Broccoli Soup 114

Instant Pot Paleo Omelet Recipes 116

Omelet with Spinach, Basil and Sausages 116

Omelet with Avocado and Chives 118

Paleo Omelet with Smoked Ham 119

Paleo Omelet with Bacon and Bell Peppers 120

Fish Omelet with Parsley 122

Salmon Omelet with Champignons and Sausages 124

Tomatoes Omelet with Cashews 125

Omelet with Turkey Sausages 127

Scrambled Eggs with Sausages and Peanuts 128

Instant Pot Paleo Fish Recipes 129

Spicy Paleo Shrimps 129

Bell Peppers with Fish and Pumpkin 131

Paleo Pike with Onions and Champignons 133

Paleo Salmon with Portobello Mushrooms 135

Paleo Fish Soup 136

Paleo Salmon Rolls with Zucchini 138

Paleo Salmon Balls with Tomato Sauce 139

Paleo Shrimps Bouillon with Pineapple 141

Shrimps Soup with Parsley 143

Carp Heads Soup with Spanish Herbs 145

Spicy Paleo Asian Soup 147

Paleo Spanish Fish Soup 149

Paleo Fish Balls 151

Fish with Almonds 152

Conclusion 154

Introduction to Paleo Diet

The Paleo diet is an ancient diet, also known as the diet of our ancestors, primitive people and tribes. During the Paleo diet, you will eat the way our ancestors ate. This diet is also called the Stone Age Diet by others. In Greek (palaios - means ancient).

Once you start following it, eating habits have to be changed permanently. The most important thing in following diet is to eat unprocessed food that is found in nature. The creators of the Paleo diet and its adherents claim to respect not only nature but also themselves by giving up all preservatives, food additives that often threaten terrible diseases: cancer, diabetes, obesity, cardiovascular diseases.

What to Eat and What Not? Consumable and Non - Consumable Food

Non Edible

When you are on the Paleo diet you should exclude: cereals and legumes, sugar and unrefined sugars, artificial sweeteners, dairy products, processed food.

Edible

And you can eat: fish and meat, eggs, vegetables, fruits, oils, seeds, various nuts. All food eaten should be as natural as possible, unprocessed, and preferably organic.

Paleo Diet Nutrition

There is more than one dietary option in the Paleo diet, but the most common is one that consists of fish, meat, a little less vegetables, then fruits, fats, and on the end there are nuts and seeds.

Most modern nutritionists and diet creators think, that the vegetables are the nutritional basis, and consider protein foods (such as meat) to cause health problems.

Proponents of the Paleo diet believe that all the food we eat causes more or less inflammation. Some products are weak, others - stronger. Because the human body is protected by immunity, it responds to all of the body's "intruders" and releases antibodies so that inflammation does not cause health problems.

When we eat fish or meat, our immunity is practically unresponsive, because animal proteins are most similar in composition to proteins found in the human body. And when eating cereals, legumes or other processed foods, the immune system understands them as foreign bodies that can potentially harm human health, and therefore devotes all its energy to protect us against these "foreign bodies." So, after eating a hearty grainy meal, we often start to feel tired, heavy and energyless.

A Sample Paleo Menu for One Day

Paleo Breakfast

The first meal of the day should be full and delicious. At the start of the day, you can pamper yourself with berries and nuts, as well as add some apples and pears. This will provide energy for the whole day.

You can eat some meat and drink a cup of coffee without sugar.

Although people on the Paleo diet did not drink coffee and tea, these products can be consumed. But, you need to feel the limits.

Paleo Lunch

Eat one apple, a piece of lean meat and drink a glass of still water.

Paleo Dinner

The dinner of a person who follows the Paleo diet consists of a salad with the vegetables flavored with the extra virgin olive oil. Also eat a piece of lean meat or fish and a glass of water.

Before Supper

You can eat the desired fruit and some of your favorite nuts so that you do not overeat before the supper.

Paleo Supper

For supper: Eat vegetable salad and oven-baked oily fish.

Before Sleep

It is not necessary to have a snack before bed, but if you really want to, eat a few nuts, an orange and drink plain water.

Instant Pot

If you think about it in the long run, we are essentially living in an age where we are completely surrounded by technology in all aspects of our life. From our day to day life, to our living rooms and even our kitchens! Smart Gadgets are taking over everything and improving the quality of life for us.

And on the topic of kitchen gadgets, the culinary industry has, in reality, undergone a significant advancement in terms of modern and new gadgets that make the process of cooking a total breeze. Appliances and gadgets such as the Sous Vide circulators, Air Fryers, Slow Cookers are designed from the ground up to make the life of rising and experienced chefs easier.

Following that very trend, the now world-famous Instant Pot came into play and completely took the whole world by storm.

In a nutshell, Instant Pots are appliances that stand at the pinnacle of Electric Pressure Cookers and completely revolutionized the cooking industry. This is the most evolved version of a traditional pressure cooker.

This cookbook includes various Instant Pot recipes with. In this cookbook, you will find interesting and mouth-watering Instant Pot recipes that will inspire you to cook delicious dishes.

Often you should just use your imagination because actually there are no limits. And remember, this cookbook hasn't all the recipes; it was created to inspire you to discover a colorful world of Instant Pot cooking!

Moreover, you don't need to be a professional 28 Michelin Star chef to use Instant Pot recipes from this cooking book and to prepare the food for yourself, your friends or your family.

So, without delaying any further, before letting you in on the recipes themselves, let me first talk a little bit about the Instant Pot itself.

About the Instant Pot

As mentioned in the section above, Instant Pot's are possibly the most advanced Electric Pressure Cookers out there. But you must be wondering, what exactly makes them so special?

Well, the Instant Pot is essentially a 7 in 1 device that has the potential to be used as a yogurt maker, food steamer, baker, gravy maker, and even a sauté pan! But that's not all to be honest, with a little bit of creativity, the list goes on.

Since the conception of the very first Instant Pot, there have been multiple models out there in the market, each designed to cater to a particular type of audience.

While the core functionalities of all of these pots remaining the same, they stand out from the group by having some model-specific features.

Below is a breakdown of some of the most common models available.

LUX

The Lux line of Instant Pot is probably the cheapest one with fewer features when compared to its bigger brothers. However, this is a good option if you are having second thoughts but still want to give the device a shot.

At the time of writing, this model had a price tag of 79$.

DUO

This is the most popular Instant Pot model that boasts a 6-quart capacity and combines the versatility of being able to have a pressure cooker, rice cooker, slow cooker, steamer, yogurt maker, Sauté/browning functionality, etc. in a single device.

There are 14 different functions in total, and the device allows you to cook at HIGH or LOW pressures, which gives you further control over your meals.

At the time of writing, this model had a price tag of 99$.

DUO PLUS

This is the updated model of the DUO and it comes packed with additional features such as Cake, Egg and Sterilize settings.

Aesthetics of the display is updated as well with a convenient blue LCD. The inner pot of the device has also seen some updates as well.

At the time of writing, this model had a price tag of 110-125$.

ULTRA

The Ultra variant of the Instant Pot comes in only 6 and 8-quart sizes. This device has a unique dial that allows you to make adjustments for custom cook settings.

Not only that! The Ultra also comes packed with a built-in altitude adjustment meter and an in-depth display, both of which helps to make the cooking process much more accessible, even in high altitude places.

At the time of writing, this model had a price tag of 149.99-159.99$.

SMART BLUETOOTH

The Smart Bluetooth variant is the most advanced Instant Pot model to date and is designed to cater to the tech enthusiasts out there.

This particular model comes packed with all the features of the Instant Pot Duo but with added Bluetooth capability.

At the time of writing, this model had a price tag of 159.99$.

How to Use the Instant Pot Buttons

Some people often think that due to the plethora of functionalities available to the Instant Pot, using the device might feel a little bit jarring and difficult.

Let me assure you now, that this is nothing more than a mere misconception! Using the Instant Pot is extremely easy and even an amateur cook can utilize it to its full potential. The only catch is that you must know what all the different buttons of the pot do.

This section is dedicated to just that. Below is a breakdown of all the core buttons of the Instant Pot, do give this is a read in order to better understand all the different functionalities of the pot itself.

Sauté: You should go for this button if you want to sauté your vegetables or meat inside your inner pot while keeping the lid open. It is possible to adjust the level of brownness you desire by pressing the modify button as well. As a small tip here, you can very quickly push the Sauté Button followed by the Adjust Button two times to simmer your food.

Keep Warm/Cancel: Using this button, you will be able to turn your pressure cooker off. Alternatively, you can use the adjust button to keep maintaining a warm temperature ranging from 293 degrees F (on average) to 332 degrees F (at more) degrees Celsius depending on what you need.

Manual: This is pretty much an all-rounder button which gives a higher level of flexibility to the user. Using this button followed by the + or – buttons, you will be able to set the exact duration of cooking time which you require.

Soup: This mode will set the cooker to a high-pressure mode giving 30 minutes of cooking time (at normal); 40 minutes (at more); 20 minutes (at less)

Meat/Stew: This mode will set the cooker to a high-pressure mode giving 35 minutes of cooking time (at normal); 45 minutes (at more); 20 minutes (at less)
Bean/Chili: This mode will set the cooker to a high-pressure mode giving 30 minutes of cooking time (at normal); 40 minutes (at more); 25 minutes (at less)

Poultry: This mode will set the cooker to a high-pressure mode giving 15 minutes of cooking time (at normal); 30 minutes (at more); 5 minutes (at less)

Rice: This is a fully automated mode that cooks rice at low pressure. It will adjust the timer all by itself depending on the amount of water/rice present in the inner cooking pot.

Multi-Grain: This mode will set the cooker to a high-pressure mode giving 40 minutes of cooking time (at normal); 45 minutes (at more); 20 minutes (at less)

Porridge: This mode will set the cooker to a high-pressure mode giving 20 minutes of cooking time (at normal); 30 minutes (at more); 15 minutes (at less)

Steam: This will set your pressure cooker to high pressure with 10 minutes of cooking time at normal. 15 minutes cook time at more and 3 minutes cook time at less. Keep in mind that it is advised to use this model with a steamer basket or rack for best results.

Slow Cooker: This button will normally set the cooker at 4-hour mode. However, you change the temperature by keeping it at 190-201 Fahrenheit (at low); 194-205 degrees Fahrenheit (at normal); 199-210 degrees Fahrenheit (at high);

Pressure: This button allows you to alter between high and low-pressure settings.

Yogurt: This setting should be used when you are in the mood for making yogurt in individual pots or jars

Timer: This button will allow you to either decrease or increase the time by using the timer button and pressing the + or – buttons.

All of the recipes in this book are made using very simple and easy to find ingredients and are perfect for small groups of 3 or 4 people. You will meat, seafood, vegetables and fish recipes in this cookbook.

But advanced chefs fear not! As in between the simpler ones, you might stumble upon a few harder recipes that will teach you a new thing or two. All said, this book essentially has something for everyone.

With that, I encourage you to start exploring the recipes and embark on your Instant Pot quest!

Instant Pot Paleo Beef Recipes

Paleo Beef Goulash with Tomato Sauce

Serving: 6

Prep Time: 15 minutes

Cooking Time: 75 minutes

Ingredients:

- 4 lb beef, cubed
- 3 tablespoons corn flour
- 3 onions, peeled and chopped
- 1 cup of tomato sauce
- 1 red bell pepper, sliced
- 1 garlic, minced
- 2 bay leaves
- 1 teaspoon cilantro
- 2 teaspoons chili powder
- 1 cup of water or beef stock
- 2 tablespoons extra virgin olive oil
- salt and pepper to taste
- 1 bunch of parsley, chopped

How to Prepare:

1. In a bowl, combine the cilantro, chili, salt, garlic and black pepper. Marinate the cubed beef in spices for at least few hours unrefrigerated at room temperature or place in the refrigerator overnight.

2. Set the Instant Pot to the sauté mode and pour few tablespoons olive oil into the pot. Spoon the cubed beef into the Instant Pot and continue cooking the meat until browned on all sides (15-20 minutes).

3. Then remove the beef meat from the Instant Pot to drain.

4. Pour the remaining oil into the pot and sauté the onions and peppers for 20 minutes until clear and caramelized. Mix in the bay leaves and chili powder.

5. Add in the beef, water or beef stock and corn flour. Pour the tomato sauce and then close the lid and cook on a MEDIUM pressure for 35 minutes. Quick-release the pressure and open the lid.

6. Then portion the beef goulash into six plates and top each plate with the parsley. Remember that this dish should be served warm. Serve the paleo beef goulash with the lettuce salad.

Nutrition (Per Serving):

Calories: 345; Fat: 64g; Carbohydrates: 244g; Protein: 52g

Instant Pot Paleo Beef Ribs in BBQ Sauce

Serving: 5

Prep Time: 12 minutes

Cook Time: 50 minutes

Ingredients:

- 5 lb beef ribs
- 1 cup of water
- 5 tablespoons BBQ sauce
- 3 medium onions, peeled and chopped
- 1 yellow pepper, peeled and diced
- 4 garlic cloves, minced
- 1 bouillon cube
- 5 tablespoons coconut oil
- 1 tablespoon chili powder
- 1 teaspoon of cayenne pepper
- 1 teaspoon of cumin

How to Prepare:

1. In a bowl, combine the garlic cloves, chili powder, cayenne pepper and cumin. Toss the beef ribs in the spices mix. Pour the

BBQ sauce on top and mix well. Then set the ribs aside to marinate for at least 10 hours in the refrigerator.

2. Set your Instant Pot to sauté mode and heat the coconut oil. Add in the onions to sauté for 10 minutes until clear and golden brown.

3. Set your Instant Pot to the WARM mode and pour the water. Then add the beef ribs, yellow pepper and bouillon cube.

4. Close the lid and cook for 50 minutes.

5. Release the pressure naturally over 10 minutes.

6. Portion the beef ribs into the five bowls or mugs and dollop each bowl with the cumin or basil. Remember that this dish should be served warm.

Nutrition (Per Serving)

Calories: 327; Fat: 52g; Carbohydrates: 238g; Protein: 40g

Paleo Beef Liver

Serving: 4

Prep Time: 10 minutes

Cooking Time: 60 minutes

Ingredients:

- 40 oz beef liver
- 1 cup of water
- 5 onions, peeled and chopped
- 5 garlic cloves, minced
- 2 tablespoons basil
- salt and pepper, to taste

How to Prepare:

1. Toss the beef liver in the minced garlic, basil, salt and pepper and marinate for around 5 hours. In the Instant Pot, pour some water and cook the beef liver on a HIGH pressure for 20 minutes.

2. In a skillet, heat the oil and simmer the onions for 10 minutes until clear and caramelized.

3. Combine the beef liver and onions in the Instant Pot. Pour some water and add some salt and pepper. Close the lid and simmer the beef liver on a LOW pressure until tender, 30 minutes.

4. Release the pressure naturally over 10 minutes.

5. Portion the beef liver into three plates. Remember that this dish should be served warm.

Nutrition (Per Serving)

Calories: 278; Fat: 41g; Carbohydrates: 265g; Protein: 38g

Paleo Beef Meatballs with Carrots

Serving: 4

Prep Time: 10 minutes

Cooking Time: 45 minutes

<u>Ingredients:</u>

- 3 lb ground beef
- 2 carrots, peeled and grated
- 1 cup of flour
- 2 eggs
- 1 teaspoon garlic powder
- 1 teaspoon onion powder
- ½ teaspoon dried oregano
- ½ teaspoon nutmeg
- 1 bunch of parsley, chopped
- 3 tablespoons extra virgin olive oil
- ¼ teaspoon each pepper and salt
- 5 tablespoons lemon juice

How to Prepare:

1. In a bowl, combine the beef meat with the carrots, basil, flour, eggs, garlic powder, onion powder, nutmeg, oregano, parsley, pepper and salt. Sprinkle some lemon juice on top and mix well. Then form 16 medium beef meatballs.

2. Pour the extra virgin olive oil into the Instant Pot and turn on the sauté mode.

3. Spoon the beef balls into the Instant Pot and simmer for 15 minutes. Continue cooking the beef balls until browned on all sides.

4. Close the lid and set the MANUAL mode. Cook on a MEDIUM pressure for 30 minutes.

5. Quick-release the pressure.

6. Portion the paleo beef meatballs into four plates and dollop each plate with the cooking liquid. Remember that this dish should be served warm.

Nutrition (Per Serving):

Calories: 375; Fat: 65g; Carbohydrates: 310g; Protein: 45g

Paleo Beef Liver with Onions

Serving: 4

Prep Time: 10 minutes

Cooking Time: 40 minutes

Ingredients:

- 3 lb beef liver, cut into pieces
- 5 tablespoons oat flour
- 3 onions, peeled and chopped
- 5 tablespoons olive oil
- ½ cup of water
- 4 teaspoons basil
- Salt and pepper, to taste
- 1 bunch of greenery, chopped

How to Prepare:

1. Marinate the beef livers in basil, salt and pepper for 1 hour in the refrigerator. Then toss the turkey liver in the oat flour.
2. Set your Instant Pot to sauté mode and add in 1 tablespoon olive oil. Spoon the onion and sauté until clear and caramelized.
3. Once the oil is hot, add the beef liver and sear both sides.
4. Then turn the sauté mode off and pour some water. Add in the salt and pepper.
5. Close the lid and cook on a MEDIUM pressure for 40 minutes.
6. Release the pressure naturally over 10 minutes. Then portion the livers into four plates and top each plate with the chopped greenery. Remember that this dish should be served warm.

Nutrition (Per Serving):

Calories: 299; Fat: 64g; Carbohydrates: 246g; Protein: 44g

Veal with Mushrooms

Serving: 4

Prep Time: 10 minutes

Cooking Time: 50 minutes

Ingredients:

- 3 lb veal, cut into pieces
- 1 cup of walnuts
- 3 tablespoons oat flour
- 5 cloves garlic, minced
- 3 tablespoons basil
- salt and pepper, to taste
- 2 tablespoons lime juice

How to Prepare:

1. Preheat the oven to 250°-270°Fahrenheit and roast the walnuts in the oven for 10 minutes until lightly browned and crispy and then set aside to cool completely. Then grind the walnuts using a food processor or blender.

2. In the Instant Pot, heat the oil and sauté the garlic for 10 minutes until clear and caramelized. Add in the basil and sauté for 10 minutes.

3. Toss the veal in the salt and pepper. Marinate the meat for around 2 hours. Then toss the veal in the flour. Place the meat into the Instant Pot. Cook the veal pieces on a MEDIUM pressure for 40 minutes.

4. Release the pressure naturally over 10 minutes.

5. Portion the veal into four plates. Sprinkle with the lime juice. Remember that this dish should be served warm.

Nutrition (Per Serving)

Calories: 324; Fat: 47g; Carbohydrates: 241g; Protein: 35g

Paleo Beef Chops with Onions and Brussels

Serving: 2

Prep Time: 10 minutes

Cooking Time: 60 minutes

Ingredients:

- 2 medium beef chops
- 1 pound Brussels sprouts
- 1 cup of walnuts
- 3 tablespoons sesame seeds oil
- ¼ teaspoon each pepper and salt
- 2 onions, peeled and chopped
- 1 bunch of greenery, chopped

How to Prepare:

1. Toss the beef chops in salt, pepper and garlic.

2. Preheat the oven to 250°-270°Fahrenheit and roast the walnuts in the oven for 5-10 minutes until lightly browned and crispy and then set aside to cool completely.

3. In the Instant Pot, select the sauté mode and simmer the onions for 10 minutes until clear and golden brown.

4. Place the beef chops, Brussels and walnuts into the Instant Pot. Pour some sesame seeds oil and close the lid to cook on a MEDIUM pressure for 40 minutes.

5. Quick-release the pressure.

6. Portion the beef into two plates and dollop each plate with the greenery. Remember that this dish should be served warm. Serve the beef chops with the salad.

Nutrition (Per Serving):

Calories: 268; Fat: 43g; Carbohydrates: 180g; Protein: 36g

Spicy Smoked Beef Clod

Serving: 4

Prep Time: 10 minute

Cook Time: 80 minutes

Ingredients:

- 3 lb beef clod
- 8 onions, peeled and chopped
- 1 cup of water
- 5 tablespoons sunflower oil
- salt and pepper to taste
- 1 tablespoon liquid smoke
- 2 teaspoons chili pepper powder
- 1 bunch of parsley

How to Prepare:

1. In a frying pan or wok, fry the onions for 15 minutes until clear and caramelized. Set your Instant Pot to sauté mode and pour some oil to heat it up.

2. Add the beef meat, salt, chili pepper powder and pepper, brown each side for 5 minutes until both sides are slightly browned.

3. Transfer them to a plate.

4. Pour the water and liquid smoke to the Instant Pot and place the meat. Spoon the onions.

5. Close the lid and cook on a HIGH pressure for about 60 minutes, release the pressure naturally over 10 minutes.

6. Transfer the beef to the cutting board and shred using 2 forks or knifes. Portion the beef into the three plates and dollop each plate with the cooking liquid. Remember that this dish should be served warm.

Nutrition (Per Serving):

Calories: 364; Fat: 75g; Carbohydrates: 266g; Protein: 61g

Spicy Paleo Beef Ribs in Sauce with Arugula

Serving: 4

Prep Time: 10 minutes

Cooking Time: 55 minutes

Ingredients:

- 3.5 lb beef ribs
- 2 cups of water
- 1 packet onion powder
- 1 bottle of spicy Buffalo sauce
- 10 oz arugula
- salt and pepper

How to Prepare:

1. In a bowl, toss the beef ribs in the onion powder. Then set the ribs aside to marinate for at least 2 hours unrefrigerated at room temperature or place in the refrigerator for 4 hours.
2. Place the steam rack inside the Instant Pot and pour some water.
3. Toss the beef ribs in the spicy Buffalo sauce.
4. Place the beef ribs on top of the rack.

5. Close the lid and cook the ribs on a HIGH pressure for 55 minutes and then release the pressure naturally over 10 minutes.

6. Remove the beef ribs from the pot and dollop each plate with the arugula and cooking liquid. Enjoy!

Nutrition (Per Serving):

Calories: 335; Fat: 88g; Carbohydrates: 252g; Protein: 55g

Bistecca alla Fiorentina Paleo Steak

Serving: 5

Prep Time: 25 minutes

Cooking Time: 50 minutes

Ingredients:

- 5 veal steaks
- 4 big onions, peeled and chopped
- 1 cup of wine
- 2 tomatoes, chopped
- 4 tablespoons garlic powder
- 1 tablespoon cilantro, chopped
- 2 tablespoons basil
- 2 teaspoons chili powder
- 3 tablespoons coconut oil
- salt and pepper to taste

How to Prepare:

1. Marinate the veal steaks in wine for at least 12 hours unrefrigerated at room temperature or place in the fridge overnight.
2. In a bowl, combine the onions, cilantro, basil, chili, salt, garlic powder and black pepper. Toss the veal steaks in the spices mix and set aside for 2 hours. Set the Instant Pot to the sauté mode and pour some oil. Add in the veal steaks and tomatoes. Close the lid and cook on a HIGH pressure for 50 minutes. Open the lid and cook the veal steaks "standing" on the side of the bone for around 10 minutes until the blood disappears from the bones.
3. Then portion the veal steaks into four plates and top each plate with the pepper. Remember that this dish should be served warm. Serve the veal with the olives.

Nutrition (Per Serving):

Calories: 348; Fat: 65g; Carbohydrates: 236g; Protein: 42g

Paleo Beef Stew

Servings: 4

Prep Time: 10 minutes

Cooking Time: 65 minutes

Ingredients:

- 4 lb beef, cubed
- 5 tablespoons Worcestershire sauce
- 4 medium onions, peeled and chopped
- 4 tablespoons white wine
- 6 cloves garlic, minced
- 3 tablespoons achiote paste
- 5 tablespoons sunflower oil
- 3 teaspoons oregano
- 1 teaspoon cumin powder
- 2 cups of chicken broth
- 2 teaspoons nutmeg
- salt and black ground pepper to taste

How to Prepare:

1. Combine the salt, nutmeg, cumin, oregano, garlic, Worcestershire sauce, achiote paste, and black pepper. Season the beef with the spices mix. Then set the beef aside to soak the meat in the marinade for at least few hours unrefrigerated at room temperature or place in the refrigerator overnight.
2. Set your Instant Pot to sauté mode and add in the Olive oil, allow the oil to heat up.
3. In the Instant Pot, sauté the chopped onions for around 10 minutes until clear and caramelized.
4. Spoon the cubed beef and stir for 5 minutes, breaking the meat. Continue cooking the meat until browned on all sides (10 minutes).
5. Then spoon all the remaining ingredients and mix well.
6. Close the lid and cook on a HIGH pressure for 50 minutes and then release the pressure over 10 minutes.
7. Serve the meat with the red wine or cold beer and chili pepper!

Nutrition (Per Serving):

Calories: 375; Fat: 75g; Carbohydrates: 267g; Protein: 65g

Paleo Beef Roulades with Dried Apricots

Serving: 3

Prep Time: 10 minutes

Cooking Time: 70 minutes

Ingredients:

- 3 lb sliced beef
- 2 cups of dried apricots, chopped
- 1 cup of onions, peeled and chopped
- 2 cups of walnuts
- 3 tablespoons sunflower oil
- 4 garlic cloves, minced

How to Prepare:

1. Preheat the oven to 240°- 250° Fahrenheit and roast the walnuts in the oven for 10 minutes until lightly browned and crispy and then set aside to cool completely. Grind the walnuts using a food processor or blender.

2. In a skillet, heat the oil and fry the onions for 10-15 minutes until clear and caramelized. Then stew for 5 minutes with the lid closed.

Add some salt and pepper. Mix well. Mix in the walnuts, garlic and apricots.

3. Spoon the filling over the beef slices. Roll the beef slices tightly encasing the filling inside. Then tie the beef roulades firmly with the kitchen twine. Add them to your instant pot and close the lid to cook on a MEDIUM pressure for 50 minutes.

4. Portion the roulades into three plates and dollop each plate with the greenery. Remember that this dish should be served warm.

Nutrition (Per Serving):

Calories: 363; Fat: 44g; Carbohydrates: 237g; Protein: 36g

Smoked Paleo Instant Beef Roast

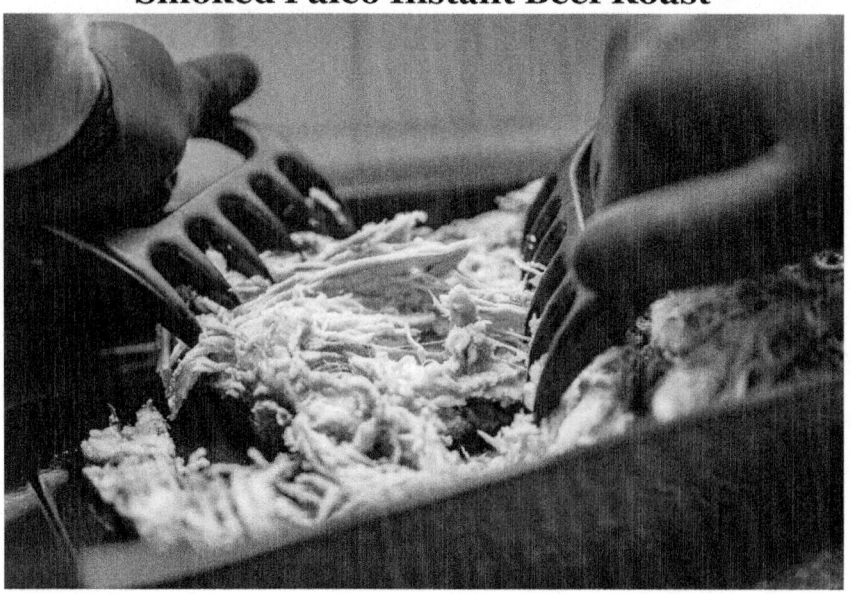

Serving: 4

Prep Time: 10 minute

Cook Time: 55 minutes

Ingredients:

- 3 lb beef
- 2 tablespoons basil
- 1 cup of water
- 5 tablespoons sunflower oil
- salt and pepper to taste
- 1 tablespoon liquid smoke
- 2 teaspoons chili pepper powder

How to Prepare:

1. Set your Instant Pot to sauté mode and pour some oil to heat it up.
2. Add the beef, salt, basil, chili pepper powder and pepper, brown each side for 5 minutes until both sides are slightly browned.
3. Pour the water and liquid smoke to the Instant Pot.

4. Close the lid and cook on a MEDIUM pressure for 50 minutes, then release the pressure naturally over 10 minutes.
5. Transfer the beef meat to the cutting board and shred using 2 forks. Portion the beef into three plates and dollop each plate with the cooking liquid. Remember that this dish should be served warm.

<u>Nutrition (Per Serving):</u>

Calories: 374; Fat: 78g; Carbohydrates: 234g; Protein: 62g

Instant Pot Paleo Pork Recipes

Paleo Pork Goulash

Serving: 5

Prep Time: 15 minutes

Cooking Time: 65 minutes

Ingredients:

- 3 lb cubed pork
- 1 cup of tomato sauce
- 2 big onions, peeled and chopped
- 3 tomatoes, chopped
- 1 red bell pepper, sliced
- 1 garlic, minced
- 2 bay leaves
- 1 teaspoon cilantro
- 2 teaspoons chili powder
- 4 cups of water or beef stock
- 2 tablespoons extra virgin olive oil
- salt and pepper to taste

How to Prepare:

1. In a bowl, combine the cilantro, chili, salt, garlic and black pepper. Marinate the cubed pork in spices for at least few hours unrefrigerated at room temperature or place in the refrigerator overnight.

2. Set the Instant Pot to the sauté mode and pour few tablespoons olive oil into the pot. Spoon the cubed pork into the Instant Pot and continue cooking the meat until browned on all sides (15-20 minutes).

3. Then remove the pork meat from the Instant Pot to drain.

4. Pour the remaining oil into the pot and sauté the onions and peppers for 20 minutes until clear and caramelized. Mix in the bay leaves and chili powder.

5. Add in the pork, water or beef stock, tomatoes, tomato sauce and close the lid. Cook on a MEDIUM pressure for 25 minutes.

6. Then portion the pork goulash into four plates and top each plate with the parsley. Remember that this dish should be served warm. Serve the paleo pork goulash with the vegetables.

Nutrition (Per Serving):

Calories: 347; Fat: 65g; Carbohydrates: 248g; Protein: 49g

Paleo Pork Stew

Servings: 6

Prep Time: 10 minutes

Cooking Time: 70 minutes

Ingredients:

- 4 lb pork, cubed
- 4 medium onions, peeled and chopped
- 6 cloves garlic, minced
- 3 tablespoons achiote paste
- 5 tablespoons coconut oil
- 2 teaspoons chili powder
- 2 chili peppers
- 3 teaspoons oregano
- 1 teaspoon cumin powder
- 2 cups of chicken broth
- 2 teaspoons nutmeg
- 1 chili, chopped
- salt and black ground pepper to taste

How to Prepare:

1. Combine salt, nutmeg, cumin, oregano, garlic, achiote paste, chili powder and black pepper. Season the pork with the spices mix. Then set the pork aside to soak the meat in the marinade for at least few hours unrefrigerated at room temperature or place in the refrigerator overnight.

2. Set your Instant Pot to sauté mode and pour the coconut oil, allow the oil to heat up.

3. In the Instant Pot, sauté the chopped onions for around 10 minutes until clear and caramelized.

4. Spoon the cubed pork and stir for 5 minutes, breaking the meat. Continue cooking the meat until browned on all sides (15 minutes).

5. Then spoon all the remaining ingredients and mix well.

6. Close the lid and cook on a HIGH pressure for 50 minutes and then release the pressure over 10 minutes.
7. Serve the meat with the beer!

Nutrition (Per Serving):

Calories: 378; Fat: 77g; Carbohydrates: 277g; Protein: 67g

Pork with BBQ Sauce and Cashews

Serving: 5

Prep Time: 10 minutes

Cooking Time: 50 minutes

Ingredients:

- 4 lb pork, diced
- 1 cup of cashews
- 1 cup of raisins
- 1 bottle of BBQ sauce
- 5 cloves garlic, minced
- 2 tablespoons basil
- salt and pepper, to taste
- 2 tablespoons lime juice

How to Prepare:

1. Preheat the oven to 250°-270°Fahrenheit and roast the cashews in the oven for 10 minutes until lightly browned and crispy and then set aside to cool completely. Then grind the cashews using a food processor or blender.
2. Marinate the pork in basil, salt, pepper and BBQ sauce for 2 hours.
3. In the Instant Pot, heat the oil and sauté the garlic for 10 minutes until clear and caramelized. Add in the pork, cashews and raisins. Sauté for 10 minutes until browned. Cook the pork on a MEDIUM pressure for 40 minutes.
4. Release the pressure naturally over 10 minutes.
5. Portion the pork into five plates. Sprinkle with the lime juice. Remember that this dish should be served warm.

Nutrition (Per Serving)

Calories: 334; Fat: 46g; Carbohydrates: 254g; Protein: 39g

Pork Chops with Ranch Dressing

Serving: 2

Prep Time: 10 minutes

Cooking Time: 40 minutes

Ingredients:

- 2 medium pork chops
- 2 tablespoons coconut oil
- 1 packet ranch mix
- 2 tablespoons garlic powder
- ¼ teaspoon each pepper and salt
- ½ cup of meat broth
- 1 bunch of greenery, chopped

How to Prepare:

1. Toss the pork chops in salt, pepper and garlic powder.
2. Heat the coconut oil in the Instant Pot and select the sauté mode to heat the oil.
3. Place the pork chops into the Instant Pot. Pour the meat broth. Close the lid and cook until brown on both sides. Cook on a MEDIUM pressure for 40 minutes.
4. 10 minutes before the pork chops are ready quick-release the pressure and open the lid. Spoon the ranch mix over the pork. Then close the lid.
5. Portion the pork into two plates and dollop each plate with the greenery. Remember that this dish should be served warm. Serve the pork chops with the salad.

Nutrition (Per Serving):

Calories: 246; Fat: 44g; Carbohydrates: 204g; Protein: 33g

Paleo Spare Ribs in BBQ Sauce

Serving: 5

Prep Time: 10 minutes

Cooking Time: 45 minutes

Ingredients:

- 4 lb pork spare ribs
- 1 cup of meat broth
- 1 packet onion powder
- 1 bottle BBQ sauce
- salt and pepper

How to Prepare:

1. In a bowl, toss the pork ribs in the onion powder. Then set the ribs aside to marinate for at least 2 hours unrefrigerated at room temperature or place in the refrigerator for 4 hours.
2. Place the steam rack inside the Instant Pot and pour some meat broth. Toss the ribs in the BBQ sauce.
3. Place the pork spare ribs on top of the rack.
4. Close the lid and cook the ribs on a HIGH pressure for 45 minutes and then release the pressure naturally over 10 minutes.
5. Remove the pork ribs from the pot and serve with the cooking liquid and remaining BBQ sauce. Enjoy!

Nutrition (Per Serving):

Calories: 330; Fat: 84g; Carbohydrates: 234g; Protein: 58g

Pork Bouillon with Celery

Serving: 4

Prep Time: 10 minutes

Cooking Time: 55 minutes

Ingredients:

- 4 lb pork, diced
- 4 tablespoon sunflower oil
- 1 bunch of dill, chopped
- 2 bay leaves
- 2 teaspoons chili pepper powder
- 1 red onion, thinly sliced
- 10 oz celery, diced
- 1 green bell pepper, thinly sliced
- 2 cloves garlic, smashed
- salt and pepper as needed
- 12 littleneck clams
- ¼ cup cilantro for garnish

How to Prepare:

1. Set your Instant Pot to sauté mode and add some sunflower oil.
2. Add the bay leaves and chili pepper powder and sauté for 5 minutes.
3. Add in the onion, bell pepper, 2 tablespoons of cilantro, garlic and season with the salt and pepper.
4. Stir for a few minutes and add in the water.
5. Spoon all the remaining ingredients to the Instant Pot.
6. Close the lid and cook on a HIGH pressure for 55 minutes.
7. Release the pressure over 10 minutes.
8. Portion the bouillon into four bowls or mugs and dollop each bowl with the chopped dill and parsley. Remember that this dish should be served warm.

Nutrition (Per Serving):

Calories: 345; Fat: 47g; Carbohydrates: 279g; Protein: 43g

Paleo Pork Rolls with Prunes and Raisins

Serving: 6

Prep Time: 10 minutes

Cooking Time: 60 minutes

Ingredients:

- 45 oz sliced pork
- 2 cups of prunes
- 4 tablespoons of raisins
- 1 cup of onions, peeled and chopped
- 1 cup of walnuts
- 3 tablespoons avocado oil
- 4 garlic cloves, minced

How to Prepare:

1. Preheat the oven to 240°- 250° Fahrenheit and roast the walnuts in the oven for 10 minutes until lightly browned and crispy and then set aside to cool completely. Grind the walnuts using a food processor or blender.

2. Soak the raisins in the warm water for 10 minutes. In the Instant Pot, heat the oil and select the sauté mode. Sauté the onions for 10 minutes until clear and caramelized.

3. In a bowl, combine the prunes, raisins, onions and walnuts. Spoon the filling over the pork slices. Roll the pork slices tightly encasing the pineapple filling inside. Then tie the pork rolls firmly with the kitchen twine. Add them to your instant pot and close the lid to cook on a MEDIUM pressure for 50 minutes.

4. Portion the pork rolls into six plates and dollop each plate with the greenery. Remember that this dish should be served warm.

Nutrition (Per Serving):

Calories: 368; Fat: 48g; Carbohydrates: 272g; Protein: 43g

Paleo Pork Rolls with Prunes and Pineapples

Serving: 5

Prep Time: 10 minutes

Cooking Time: 50 minutes

Ingredients:

- 4 lb pork, sliced
- 2 cups of prunes, chopped
- 1 cup of pineapple, diced
- 1 cup of onions, peeled and chopped
- 1 cup of walnuts
- 3 tablespoons extra virgin olive oil
- 4 garlic cloves, minced
- 1 bunch of greenery

How to Prepare:

1. Preheat the oven to 240°- 250° Fahrenheit and roast the walnuts in the oven for 10 minutes until lightly browned and crispy and then set aside to cool completely. Grind the walnuts using a food processor or blender.

2. In a bowl, combine the prunes, pineapple cubes, onions and walnuts. Spoon the filling over the pork slices. Roll the pork slices tightly encasing the pineapple filling inside. Then tie the pork rolls firmly with the kitchen twine. Add it to your instant pot and close the lid to cook on a MEDIUM pressure for 50 minutes.

3. Portion the pork rolls into four plates and dollop each plate with the greenery. Remember that this dish should be served warm.

Nutrition (Per Serving):

Calories: 288; Fat: 42g; Carbohydrates: 251g; Protein: 42g

Paleo Instant Pork with Peanuts

Serving: 5

Prep Time: 15 minutes

Cooking Time: 45 minutes

Ingredients:

- 45 oz pork, ground
- ½ big onion, chopped
- 2 cups of peanuts
- 1 garlic clove, minced
- 1 bay leaf
- 2 ounces tomato sauce
- 4 tablespoons coconut oil
- 1 tablespoon cilantro, chopped
- ½ cup of water
- 2 teaspoon chili powder
- Salt and pepper, to taste
- 1 bunch of parsley, chopped

How to Prepare:

1. Preheat the oven to 240°-260° Fahrenheit and roast the peanuts in the oven for 10 minutes until lightly browned and crispy and then set aside to cool completely. Then grind the peanuts using a food processor or blender.
2. Marinate the pork in the salt, pepper, cilantro and chili powder for at least few hours unrefrigerated at room temperature or place in the fridge overnight. Set the Instant Pot to sauté mode and pour the coconut oil. Heat the oil and add in the pork. Break the pork meat into pieces and cook until browned.
3. Add in all the minced garlic, bay leaf, tomato sauce, peanuts, onion and pour some water. Mix well.
4. Close the lid and cook on a MEDIUM pressure for 45 minutes.
5. Then portion the pork into five plates or bowls and dollop each plate with the chopped parsley. Remember that this dish should be served warm. Serve it with the salad.

Nutrition (Per Serving):

Calories: 383; Fat: 82g; Carbohydrates: 284g; Protein: 72g

Paleo Spicy Pork Ribs with Bell Peppers

Serving: 4

Prep Time: 10 minutes

Cooking Time: 65 minutes

Ingredients:

- 40 oz short pork ribs, 4 inches thick, cut into 3 rib portions
- 1 bottle of beer
- 5 bell peppers, diced
- 4 medium onions, peeled and chopped
- 5 garlic cloves, smashed
- 2 quarter-sized ginger slices
- 1 cup of water
- 5 tablespoons sesame oil
- 3 teaspoons chili powder
- salt and pepper

How to Prepare:

1. In a bowl, combine the chili powder, salt, garlic and black pepper. Season the pork ribs with the spices mix and pour the beer over the meat. Then set the ribs aside to marinate for at least 12

hours unrefrigerated at room temperature or place in the fridge for 24 hours.
2. Set your Instant Pot to sauté mode and add in the sesame oil, let it shimmer.
3. Mix in the onions, bell peppers and ginger to sauté for 10 minutes until clear and caramelized.
4. Add in the short ribs, water, sesame oil, and stir until the ribs are coated well. Close the lid and cook on a HIGH pressure for 55 minutes and then release the pressure naturally over 10 minutes.
5. Remove the short ribs from the pot and serve with the cooking liquid and onions. Enjoy!

Nutrition (Per Serving):

Calories: 327; Fat: 84g; Carbohydrates: 223g; Protein: 49g

Napa Cabbage with Sausages and Carrots

Serving: 5

Prep Time: 10 minutes

Cooking Time: 60 minutes

Ingredients:

- 6 pork sausages, cut into rings
- 1 medium napa cabbage, chopped
- 3 carrots, peeled and sliced
- 4 tablespoons dried sage
- 2 tablespoons sunflower oil
- 2 teaspoons dried thyme
- 2 teaspoons ground cinnamon
- 1 cup of chicken broth
- 1 teaspoon of salt
- 1 teaspoon pepper

How to Prepare:

1. First, set your Instant Pot to sauté mode and add in the sunflower oil. Sauté the sausages for 10 minutes and then spoon the sausages into your Instant Pot.

2. In a bowl, combine the salt, pepper, dried thyme, sage and cinnamon. Add them to the Instant Pot.
3. Then, add in the napa cabbage and carrots and pour in the chicken broth.
4. Close the lid and cook on a HIGH pressure for about 50 minutes.
5. Quick-release the pressure and transfer the sausages to a plate.
6. Spoon the napa cabbage and the sausages and ladle up the sauce (if any) all over the sausages. Serve with the cold beer.

Nutrition (Per Serving):

Calories: 342; Fat: 79g; Carbohydrates: 266g; Protein: 62g

Spicy Pork Ribs with Mango

Serving: 4

Prep Time: 10 minutes

Cook Time: 55 minutes

Ingredients:

- 20 oz pork ribs
- 2 cups of mango, diced
- 3 cups of water
- 5 tablespoons tomato sauce
- 3 medium onions, peeled and chopped
- 1 yellow pepper, peeled and diced
- 4 garlic cloves, minced
- 1 bouillon cube
- 2 tablespoons sunflower oil
- 1 tablespoon chili powder
- 1 teaspoon of cayenne pepper
- 1 teaspoon of cumin
- 2 cucumbers, sliced

How to Prepare:

1. In a bowl, combine the garlic cloves, chili powder, cayenne pepper and cumin. Toss the pork ribs in the spices mix. Then set the pork aside to marinate for at least few hours unrefrigerated at room temperature or place in the fridge overnight.
2. Set your Instant Pot to sauté mode and pour some sunflower oil. Add in the garlic and onions, to sauté for 5 minutes until clear and caramelized.
3. Set your Instant Pot to the WARM mode and add in all the remaining ingredients.
4. Close the lid and cook on a HIGH pressure for 40 minutes.
5. Release the pressure naturally over 10 minutes.
6. Portion the pork ribs into four bowls or mugs and dollop each bowl with the cumin and sliced cucumbers. Remember that this dish should be served warm.

Nutrition (Per Serving)

Calories: 312; Fat: 48g; Carbohydrates: 245g; Protein: 37g

Jamaican Jerk Pork Roast

Serving: 3

Prep Time: 10 minutes

Cooking Time: 40 minutes

Ingredients:

- 3 lb pork shoulder
- 2 tablespoons extra virgin olive oil
- 1 packet Jamaican Jerk spice blend
- ¼ teaspoon each pepper and salt
- ½ cup of meat broth
- 1 bunch of greenery, chopped

How to Prepare:

1. Pour the extra virgin olive oil over the pork shoulder. Toss the pork shoulder in Jamaican Jerk spice blend, salt and pepper.
2. Heat the Instant Pot and select the sauté mode.
3. Place the pork shoulder into the Instant Pot. Pour the meat broth. Close the lid and cook on a MEDIUM pressure for 40 minutes.
4. Quick-release the pressure and open the lid. Place the pork shoulder on a plate and shred the pork using 2 forks.
5. Portion the pork into three plates and dollop each plate with the greenery. Remember that this dish should be served warm. Serve the pork shoulder with the salad.

Nutrition (Per Serving):

Calories: 349; Fat: 47g; Carbohydrates: 264g; Protein: 39g

Pork Ribs with Celery in Honey

Serving: 3

Prep Time: 10 minutes

Cooking Time: 50 minutes

Ingredients:

- 35 oz pork ribs
- 20 oz celery
- 1 cup of walnuts
- 5 tablespoons honey
- 2 teaspoons sesame oil
- 4 tablespoons soya sauce
- 1 teaspoon salt
- 1 cup of water
- ½ cup of liquid smoke

How to Prepare:

1. Preheat the oven to 240°-260°Fahrenheit and roast the walnuts in the oven for 10 minutes until lightly browned and crispy and then set aside to cool completely. Then grind the walnuts using a food processor or blender.

2. In a bowl, marinate the pork ribs in honey. Then set the pork aside to marinate it for at least few hours unrefrigerated at room temperature or place in the fridge overnight.
3. Open the lid and pour the sesame oil. Set the Instant Pot to the sauté mode and heat the oil. Add the pork, celery, soya sauce, salt, water and liquid smoke to the Instant Pot.
4. Close the lid and cook on a MEAT/STEW mode for 50 minutes. Release the pressure naturally over 10 minutes.
5. Portion the pork ribs into three plates and dollop each plate with the cooking liquid and soya sauce. Remember that this dish should be served warm. Serve it with the green vegetables on the side if you prefer.

Nutrition (Per Serving):

Calories: 329; Fat: 73g; Carbohydrates: 265g; Protein: 59g

Paleo Pork Roulades with Apricots

Serving: 4

Prep Time: 10 minutes

Cooking Time: 60 minutes

Ingredients:

- 40 oz sliced pork
- 1 cup of dried apricots, chopped
- 1 cup of onions, peeled and chopped
- 1 cup of peanuts
- 3 tablespoons sunflower oil
- 4 garlic cloves, minced

How to Prepare:

1. Preheat the oven to 240°- 250° Fahrenheit and roast the peanuts in the oven for 10 minutes until lightly browned and crispy and then set aside to cool completely. Grind the peanuts using a food processor or blender.

2. In a skillet, heat the oil and simmer the onions for 10-15 minutes until clear and caramelized. Add the peanuts, apricots, salt and pepper. Mix well.

3. Spoon the filling over the pork slices. Roll the pork slices tightly encasing the filling inside. Then tie the pork roulades firmly with the kitchen twine. Add them to your instant pot and close the lid to cook on a MEDIUM pressure for 45 minutes.

4. Portion the pork roulades into four plates. Remember that this dish should be served warm.

Nutrition (Per Serving):

Calories: 297; Fat: 54g; Carbohydrates: 207g; Protein: 44g

Bacon and Pancetta in Lime Juice

Serving: 4

Prep Time: 15 minutes

Cooking Time: 50 minutes

Ingredients:

- 6 pieces 2-inch bacon
- 5 tablespoons lime juice
- 4 ounces pancetta, diced
- 2 medium shallots, chopped
- 5 garlic cloves, minced
- 3 teaspoons dried rosemary
- 2 teaspoons black pepper
- 1 teaspoon nutmeg
- 1 cup of chicken broth

How to Prepare:

1. In a bowl, combine the black pepper, dried rosemary, nutmeg and garlic. Toss the bacon in the spices mix and pour the lime juice on top. Then set the bacon aside to marinate it for at least few hours unrefrigerated at room temperature or place in the fridge overnight.
2. Set your pot to sauté mode and add in the pancetta to cook for about 5 minutes.
3. Then transfer the browned up pancetta to a plate.
4. Add shallots and cook for 5 minutes.
5. Combine all the ingredients in you Instant Pot and close the lid to let them cook on a HIGH pressure for about 40 minutes.
6. Release the pressure and place the bacon to a carving board.
7. Slice up the meat into strips and then divide into four bowls or plates and ladle up the tomato sauce on top to serve with the vegetables and wine.

Nutrition (Per Serving):

Calories: 342; Fat: 82g; Carbohydrates: 284g; Protein: 78g

Paleo Pork Rinds

Serving: 1

Prep Time: 10 minutes

Cooking Time: 50 minutes

Ingredients:

- 20 oz pork, sliced
- ½ can canned corns
- 2 carrots, peeled and diced
- ½ can canned peas
- ½ cup vegetables broth
- 4 tablespoons Olive oil
- 1 teaspoon chili pepper powder
- 5 tablespoons lime juice

How to Prepare:

1. Pour some Olive oil over the pork. Then sprinkle the lime juice on all sides and marinate the pork for at least few hours unrefrigerated at room temperature or place in the fridge overnight. Set your Instant Pot to sauté mode.
2. Pour some oil and add in the pork. Brown the pork on all sides for around 10-15 minutes.
3. Then pour the vegetables broth over the pork and mix in the remaining ingredients.
4. Close the lid and cook on a HIGH pressure for 35 minutes.
5. Release the pressure naturally over 10 minutes.
6. Portion the pork into the plate and dollop each plate with the lime juice.

Nutrition (Per Serving):

Calories: 359; Fat: 75g; Carbohydrates: 262g; Protein: 56g

Instant Pot Paleo Chicken, Turkey and Goose Recipes

Paleo Chicken Breast with Cheese

Serving: 3

Prep Time: 10 minutes

Cooking Time: 30 minutes

Ingredients:

- 3 lb chicken breast, sliced
- 2 avocados, halved
- 4 tablespoons coconut oil
- 2 tablespoons garlic powder
- 1 teaspoon chili powder
- ¼ teaspoon each pepper and salt
- 10 oz Vegan cheese, grated

How to Prepare:

1. Toss the chicken breast in salt, pepper, garlic powder and chili powder.

2. Heat the coconut oil in the Instant Pot and select the sauté mode to heat the oil.
3. Place the chicken breast slices into the Instant Pot. Close the lid and cook on a MEDIUM pressure for 30 minutes.
4. Quick-release the pressure and open the lid.
5. Portion the chicken breast into three plates and dollop each plate with the Vegan cheese. Remember that this dish should be served warm. Serve the chicken breast with the avocado halves.

Nutrition (Per Serving):

Calories: 278; Fat: 36g; Carbohydrates: 185g; Protein: 32g

Paleo Chicken Rolls with Carrots

Serving: 4

Prep Time: 10 minutes

Cooking Time: 65 minutes

Ingredients:

- 30 oz sliced chicken
- 4 carrots, peeled and chopped
- 2 onions, peeled and chopped
- 1 cup of mayonnaise
- 3 tablespoons avocado oil
- 4 garlic cloves, minced

How to Prepare:

1. Set the Instant Pot to the sauté mode and pour the avocado oil. Then heat the oil. Spoon the carrots, onions and garlic. Sauté for 15 minutes until clear and caramelized.

2. In a bowl, combine the carrots, onions, garlic and mayonnaise. Spoon the filling over the chicken slices. Roll the chicken slices tightly encasing the filling inside. Then tie the chicken rolls firmly with the kitchen twine. Add them to your Instant Pot and close the lid to cook on a MEDIUM pressure for 50 minutes.

3. Portion the chicken rolls into four plates and dollop each plate with the greenery. Remember that this dish should be served warm.

Nutrition (Per Serving):

Calories: 318; Fat: 43g; Carbohydrates: 237g; Protein: 35g

Paleo Goose with Pumpkin

Serving: 4

Prep Time: 10 minutes

Cooking Time: 60 minutes

Ingredients:

- 1 goose, cut into pieces
- 10 oz pumpkin, sliced
- 2 glasses of beer
- 5 tablespoons olive oil
- 1 tablespoon of Italian seasoning
- 4 tablespoons sunflower oil
- 1 cup of water
- 4 teaspoons basil
- Salt and pepper, to taste
- 1 bunch of greenery, chopped

How to Prepare:

1. Marinate the goose in beer for 10 hours in the refrigerator.

2. Set your Instant Pot to sauté mode and add in 1 tablespoon Olive oil.
3. Once the oil is hot, add the goose pieces and sear both sides. Spoon some salt and pepper.
4. Then turn the sauté mode off and pour the water. Add in the Italian seasoning mix, salt, pepper and basil on top of your goose.
5. Close the lid and cook on a MEDIUM pressure for 50 minutes.
6. Release the pressure naturally over 10 minutes.
7. Then portion the goose into four plates and top each plate with the chopped greenery. Remember that this dish should be served warm.

Nutrition (Per Serving):

Calories: 281; Fat: 66g; Carbohydrates: 215g; Protein: 45g

Paleo Goose with Apples, Prunes and Apricots

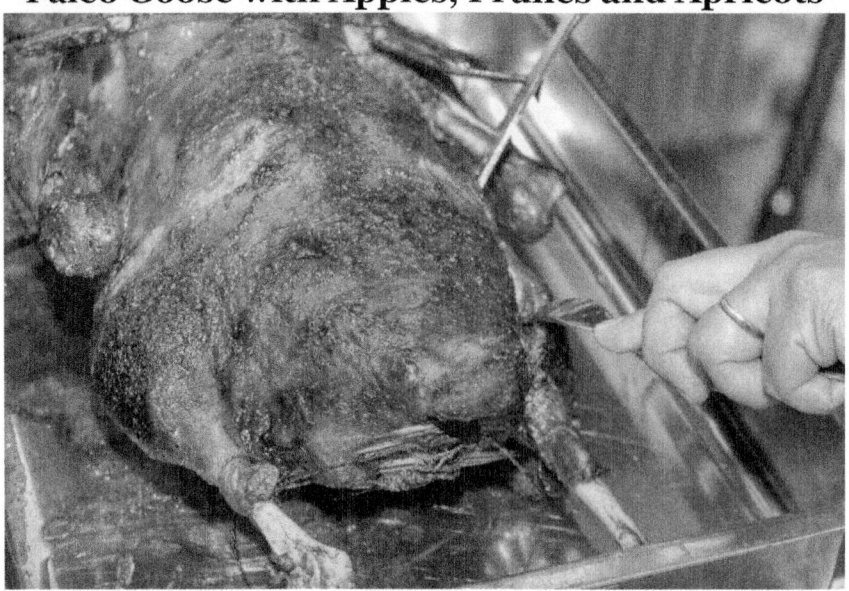

Serving: 4

Prep Time: 10 minutes

Cooking Time: 50 minutes

Ingredients:

- 1 medium goose
- 2 cups of apricots
- 1 cup of prunes
- 5 apples, diced
- 1 cup of peanuts
- 3 tablespoons sunflower oil
- 1 teaspoon each pepper and salt
- 5 garlic cloves, minced
- 1 bunch of greenery, chopped

How to Prepare:

1. Toss the goose carcass in salt, pepper and garlic and marinate for few hours.

2. Preheat the oven to 250°-270°Fahrenheit and roast the peanuts in the oven for 5-10 minutes until lightly browned and crispy and then set aside to cool completely.

3. Stuff the goose with the apricots, prunes, apples and peanuts. Place the goose into the Instant Pot. Pour some sunflower oil and close the lid to cook on a MEDIUM pressure for 50 minutes.

4. Quick-release the pressure.

5. Portion the goose into four plates and dollop each plate with the greenery. Remember that this dish should be served warm. Serve the goose with the lettuce.

Nutrition (Per Serving):

Calories: 295; Fat: 55g; Carbohydrates: 225g; Protein: 49g

Paleo Salsa Chicken

Serving: 3

Prep Time: 10 minutes

Cooking Time: 40 minutes

Ingredients:

- 2.5 chicken breast
- 2 cups of salsa
- 1 cup of chicken stock
- 2 tsp. taco seasoning
- 2 medium mangos, diced
- 1 avocado, diced
- 2 medium carrots, peeled and diced
- Salt and pepper, to taste
- 1 garlic, minced

How to Prepare:

1. Toss the chicken breast in the minced garlic, salt and pepper and marinate for around 2 hours.

2. Combine the chicken steaks, carrots and mangos in the Instant Pot. Pour the chicken stock. Set the poultry mode and close the lid. Cook for 20 minutes.

3. Transfer the chicken to a plate and shred it using two forks. Then place the chicken back into the Instant Pot and spoon all the remaining ingredients. Set to the sauté mode and cook for 20 minutes.

4. Release the pressure naturally over 10 minutes.

5. Portion the chicken breast into the plates. Remember that this dish should be served warm with the sliced tomatoes.

Nutrition (Per Serving)

Calories: 245; Fat: 45g; Carbohydrates: 184g; Protein: 39g

Paleo Turkey Steaks

Serving: 2

Prep Time: 10 minutes

Cooking Time: 35 minutes

Ingredients:

- 2 turkey steaks
- 2 onions, chopped
- ½ cup of water
- Salt and pepper, to taste
- 2 tablespoons extra virgin olive oil
- 5 cloves garlic, minced
- 1 teaspoon nutmeg
- 1 teaspoon basil
- 2 bay leaves (Laurus nobilis)

How to Prepare:

1. Marinate the turkey steaks in salt, pepper and garlic for few hours.
2. In the Instant Pot, heat the olive oil and sauté the onions on a low heat for around 5 minutes until clear and caramelized.

3. Add the turkey steaks and spices to the Instant Pot. Pour some water. Close the lid and cook on a MEDIUM pressure for 30 minutes.
4. Release the pressure naturally over 10 minutes.
5. Portion the turkey steaks into two plates. Remember that this dish should be served warm with the vegetable salad.

Nutrition (Per Serving)

Calories: 184; Fat: 27g; Carbohydrates: 129g; Protein: 26g

Paleo Goose Curry with Broccoli

Serving: 2

Prep Time: 10 minutes

Cooking Time: 50 minutes

Ingredients:

- 1 medium goose, cut into pieces
- 1 tablespoon curry powder
- 2 tablespoons onion powder
- 2 tablespoons garlic powder
- 4 teaspoons basil
- Salt and pepper, to taste

Curry:

- 2 tablespoons curry powder
- 1 cup of chicken broth
- 2 cups of coconut milk
- 3 cups of broccoli florets
- 1 tablespoon sugar

How to Prepare:

1. Combine the goose with the salt, basil, pepper and curry. Mix well. Marinate the goose for few hours in the refrigerator.

2. Set your Instant Pot to sauté mode and add in 1 tablespoon Olive oil.

3. Once the oil is hot, add the goose pieces and sear both sides.

4. Then turn the sauté mode off and pour the chicken broth and coconut milk. Add in the curry powder, sugar and broccoli florets.

5. Close the lid and cook on a MEDIUM pressure for 50 minutes.

6. Release the pressure naturally over 10 minutes.

7. Then portion the goose into two plates and top each plate with the basil. Remember that this dish should be served warm. Serve it with the red or white wine.

Nutrition (Per Serving):

Calories: 356; Fat: 73g; Carbohydrates: 236g; Protein: 53g

Paleo Keema Chicken with Zucchini

Serving: 4

Prep Time: 10 minutes

Cooking Time: 45 minutes

Ingredients:

- 2 lb chicken, ground
- 1 medium zucchini, spiralized
- 5 medium tomatoes, diced
- 2 onions, peeled and chopped
- 1 tablespoon ghee
- 1 tablespoon ginger
- 1 cup of peanuts
- 3 tablespoons soy sauce
- 1 tablespoon turmeric
- 1 tablespoon cumin powder
- 1 teaspoon paprika
- 1 teaspoon garam masala
- 1 cup of water
- 2 teaspoons salt
- Serrano pepper, minced
- 1 tablespoon coriander powder
- fresh parsley

How to Prepare:

1. In the Instant Pot, combine the ghee and the onions. Sauté for 10 minutes until clear and caramelized. Then mix in the ginger, turmeric, cumin powder, paprika, garam masala, salt, Serrano pepper and coriander powder.
2. Preheat the oven to 250°-270°Fahrenheit and roast the peanuts in the oven for 10 minutes until lightly browned and crispy and then set aside to cool completely. Then grind the peanuts using a food processor or blender. Cook for 5 minutes.
3. Add in the chicken and sauté for 15 minutes until brown.

4. Mix in the zucchini, tomatoes, peanuts, soy sauce and pour some water. Close the lid to cook on MEAT/STEW mode. Set the timer to 45 minutes.
5. Release the pressure over 10 minutes.
6. Serve the chicken meat with the fresh parsley and enjoy!

<u>Nutrition (Per Serving):</u>

Calories: 311; Fat: 68g; Carbohydrates: 241g; Protein: 58g

Paleo Chicken Wings with Walnuts

Servings: 4

Prep Time: 20 minutes

Cooking Time: 65 minutes

Ingredients:

- 30 oz chicken wings
- 1 cup of walnuts
- 4 oranges, peeled and diced
- 2 medium onions, peeled and chopped
- 6 cloves garlic, minced
- 2 teaspoons chili powder
- 3 teaspoons oregano
- 1 teaspoon cumin powder
- 5 tablespoons extra virgin olive oil
- 2 cups of tomatoes, chopped
- 2 cups of chicken broth
- 2 teaspoons nutmeg
- Salt and pepper to taste

How to Prepare:

1. Preheat the oven to 250°-270°Fahrenheit and roast the walnuts in the oven for 10 minutes until lightly browned and crispy and then set aside to cool completely. Then grind the nuts using a food processor or blender.

2. Combine the salt, nutmeg, cumin, oregano, garlic, pistachios and black pepper. Season the chicken wings with the spices mix. Spoon the diced oranges and mix well. Then set the chicken wings aside to marinate for at least few hours unrefrigerated at room temperature.

3. In a skillet or wok, heat the olive oil and fry the chopped onions for around 10 minutes until clear and caramelized.

4. Set your Instant Pot to sauté mode and add in the olive oil to heat it up.

5. Spoon the chicken wings and simmer for 5 minutes. Mix in the onions and sauté until fragrant, then spoon all the remaining ingredients and mix well.

6. Close the lid and cook on a MEDIUM pressure for 40 minutes and then release the pressure over 10 minutes.

7. Serve with the cucumbers and tomato sauce.

Nutrition (Per Serving):

Calories: 360; Fat: 74g; Carbohydrates: 259g; Protein: 52g

Turkey with Pumpkin Puree and Tomatoes

Serving: 2

Prep Time: 15 minute

Cooking Time: 55 minutes

Ingredients:

- 3 lb turkey, diced
- 5 pounds small-sized pumpkin, seeded and diced
- 20 oz tomatoes, diced
- 5 onions, peeled and chopped
- 4 tablespoons coconut oil
- 1 cup of water
- Salt and pepper to taste
- 1 bunch of greenery, chopped

How to Prepare:

1. Add the water to your Instant Pot and place the diced pumpkin and close the lid to cook on a HIGH pressure for 15-20 minutes.
2. Quick-release the pressure and let the pumpkin to cool.
3. Then, scoop out the flesh into a bowl.
4. In the Instant Pot, heat the oil and then sauté turkey, pumpkin, onions and tomatoes for 35 minutes until golden brown.
5. Portion the turkey into two bowls or mugs and dollop each bowl with the greenery. Remember that this dish should be served warm.

Nutrition (Per Serving):

Calories: 171; Fat: 49g; Carbohydrates: 256g; Protein: 38g

Baked Paleo Chicken Drumsticks

Serving: 2

Prep Time: 10 minutes

Cooking Time: 30 minutes

Ingredients:

- 6 chicken legs
- 2 tablespoons coconut oil
- 2 tablespoons garlic powder
- 2 tablespoons onion powder
- 1 tablespoon smoked paprika
- ¼ teaspoon each pepper and salt
- 4 tablespoons extra virgin olive oil

How to Prepare:

1. Mix together garlic powder, onion powder, smoked paprika, salt and pepper.
2. Toss the chicken legs in this mix.
3. Pour some olive oil into the Instant Pot. Select the sauté mode and heat the extra virgin olive oil in the Instant Pot.

4. Place the chicken drumsticks into the Instant Pot. Close the lid and cook until brown on both sides. Cook on a MEDIUM pressure for 30 minutes.

5. Quick-release the pressure and open the lid.

6. Portion the chicken legs into two plates and dollop each plate with the greenery. Remember that this dish should be served warm. Serve the chicken drumsticks with the salad.

Nutrition (Per Serving):

Calories: 246; Fat: 42g; Carbohydrates: 202g; Protein: 31g

Paleo Turkey Roulades with Prunes and Raisins

Serving: 4

Prep Time: 10 minutes

Cooking Time: 55 minutes

Ingredients:

- 35 oz turkey, sliced
- 1 cup of prunes, chopped
- 1 cup of raisins
- 1 cup of onions, peeled and chopped
- 2 cups of walnuts
- 3 tablespoons sunflower oil
- 4 garlic cloves, minced
- Salt, to taste

How to Prepare:

1. Preheat the oven to 240°- 250° Fahrenheit and roast the walnuts in the oven for 10 minutes until lightly browned and crispy and then set aside to cool completely. Grind the walnuts using a food processor or blender.

2. In the Instant Pot, heat the oil and simmer the onions for 10-15 minutes until clear and caramelized. Add some walnuts, prunes, raisins and some salt. Mix well.

3. Spoon the filling over the turkey slices. Roll the turkey slices tightly encasing the filling inside. Then tie the turkey roulades firmly with the kitchen twine. Add them to your instant pot and close the lid to cook on a MEDIUM pressure for 40 minutes.

4. Portion the roulades into four plates. Remember that this dish should be served warm.

Nutrition (Per Serving):

Calories: 241; Fat: 35g; Carbohydrates: 178g; Protein: 27g

French Goose with Oranges and Peanuts

Serving: 4

Prep Time: 10 minutes

Cook Time: 55 minutes

Ingredients:

- 1 goose, cut into pieces
- 1 cup of peanuts
- 2 oranges, halved
- 2 carrots, peeled and diced
- 2 tablespoons soy sauce
- 1 tablespoon dry basil
- 5 garlic cloves, minced
- 4 tablespoons olive oil
- 2-3 teaspoons salt
- 1 cup of water

How to Prepare:

1. Preheat the oven to 240°-260° Fahrenheit and roast the peanuts in the oven for 10 minutes until lightly browned and crispy and then set aside to cool completely. Then grind the peanuts using a food processor or blender.

2. Marinate the goose pieces in the salt, soy sauce, dry basil, minced garlic and lemons for at least few hours unrefrigerated at room temperature or place in the fridge overnight.

3. Add in the marinated goose and all the listed ingredients to your Instant Pot. Close the lid and set the timer to 45 minutes and cook the duck on MEAT/STEW mode.

4. Release the pressure naturally over 10 minutes.

5. Portion the goose into four plates and dollop each plate with the cooking liquid and soya sauce. Remember that this dish should be served warm. Serve the goose with the brown rice on the side if you prefer.

Nutrition (Per Serving):

Calories: 358; Fat: 62g; Carbohydrates: 267g; Protein: 58g

Instant Goose in Spices

Serving: 3

Prep Time: 10 minutes

Cook Time: 45 minutes

Ingredients:

- 1 goose, cut into pieces
- 2 carrots, peeled and diced
- 10 oz celery, diced
- 2 tablespoons soy sauce
- 1 tablespoon dry basil
- 2 tablespoons cilantro
- 2 tablespoons rosemary
- 2 tablespoons oregano
- 2 tablespoons thyme
- 5 garlic cloves, minced
- 4 tablespoons olive oil
- 2-3 teaspoons salt
- 1 cup of water

How to Prepare:

1. Toss the goose pieces in the salt, soy sauce, 1 tablespoon dry basil, minced garlic, 2 tablespoons cilantro, 2 tablespoons rosemary, 2 tablespoons oregano, 2 tablespoons thyme. Marinate the goose for at least 10 hours in the refrigerator.
2. Add in the marinated goose and all the listed ingredients to your Instant Pot. Close the lid and set the timer to 55 minutes and cook the goose on MEAT/STEW mode.
3. Release the pressure naturally over 10 minutes.
4. Portion the goose into three plates and dollop each plate with the cooking liquid and soya sauce. Remember that this dish should be served warm. Serve the goose with the vegetables on the side if you prefer.

Nutrition (Per Serving):

Calories: 323; Fat: 61g; Carbohydrates: 262g; Protein: 53g

Turkey Chunks with Walnuts

Serving: 3

Prep Time: 20 minutes

Cook Time: 50 minutes

Ingredients:

- 28 oz (1 can) turkey chunks with broth, canned
- 4 medium onions, peeled and sliced
- 1 cup of walnuts
- 3 cups of water
- ½ teaspoon salt and pepper

How to Prepare:

1. Preheat the oven to 250°-270°Fahrenheit and roast the walnuts in the oven for 10 minutes until lightly browned and crispy and then set aside to cool completely. Then grind the walnuts using a food processor or blender.

2. In a skillet or wok, fry the onions for 10 minutes until clear and caramelized. In a bowl, mash the turkey meat using a fork.

3. Combine the water, turkey chunks and caramelized onions and add to your Instant Pot.

4. Close the lid and cook on a HIGH pressure for 30 minutes.

5. Release the pressure naturally over 10 minutes.

6. Portion the turkey chunks into three bowls or mugs and dollop each bowl with the walnuts, salt and pepper. Remember that this dish should be served warm. Serve the turkey chunks with the fresh vegetable salad.

Nutrition (Per Serving)

Calories: 178; Fat: 31g; Carbohydrates: 127g; Protein: 27g

Paleo Chicken with Pineapples and Apples

Serving: 4

Prep Time: 10 minutes

Cook Time: 65 minutes

Ingredients:

- 40 oz chicken
- 2 cups of cashews
- 2 cups of pineapples, diced
- 5 apples, peeled and diced
- 5 tablespoons herbs
- 2 tablespoons soy sauce
- 1 tablespoon dry basil
- 5 garlic cloves, minced
- 4 tablespoons olive oil
- Salt as needed
- 1 cup of freshly squeezed orange juice
- ½ tablespoon of corn starch
- ½ cup of water

How to Prepare:

1. Preheat the oven to 240°-260°Fahrenheit and roast the cashews in the oven for 10 minutes until lightly browned and crispy and then set aside to cool completely. Then grind the cashews using a food processor or blender.

2. Marinate the chicken in the salt, soy sauce, dry basil, minced garlic, orange juice and herbs for at least few hours unrefrigerated at room temperature or place in the fridge overnight. Add the marinated chicken and all the listed ingredients to your Instant Pot.

3. Close the lid and set the timer to 55 minutes and cook the chicken on MEAT/STEW mode.

4. Release the pressure naturally over 10 minutes.

5. Serve and enjoy!

Nutrition (Per Serving):

Calories: 304; Fat: 70g; Carbohydrates: 242g; Protein: 53g

Paleo Turkey with Squash

Serving: 3

Prep Time: 10 minutes

Cooking Time: 50 minutes

Ingredients:

- 20 oz turkey meat, cubed
- 20 oz squash, peeled and diced
- 4 tablespoons dried sage
- 2 teaspoons dried thyme
- 2 teaspoons ground cinnamon
- 1 cup of chicken broth
- 2 tablespoons sunflower oil
- 1 teaspoon of salt
- 1 teaspoon pepper

How to Prepare:

1. First, set your Instant Pot to sauté mode and pour some oil. In a skillet, fry the cubed turkey for 20 minutes until golden brown and then spoon the turkey into your Instant Pot.
2. Mix in the salt, pepper, dried thyme, sage and cinnamon.
3. Then, add in the squash and pour in the chicken broth.
4. Close the lid and cook on a MEDIUM pressure for about 30 minutes.
5. Quick-release the pressure and transfer the turkey to a plate.
6. Spoon the turkey and squash into the plates and ladle up the sauce (if any) all over the turkey. Serve it with the white wine.

Nutrition (Per Serving):

Calories: 269; Fat: 54g; Carbohydrates: 221g; Protein: 39g

Paleo Chicken with Apples

Serving: 3

Prep Time: 10 minutes

Cooking Time: 50 minutes

Ingredients:

- 1 medium chicken carcass
- 5 sour apples, diced
- 2 cups of prunes
- 1 cup of peanuts
- 3 tablespoons sunflower oil
- 1 teaspoon each pepper and salt
- 5 garlic cloves, minced
- 1 bunch of greenery, chopped

How to Prepare:

1. Toss the chicken carcass in salt, pepper and garlic and marinate for few hours.

2. Preheat the oven to 250°-270°Fahrenheit and roast the peanuts in the oven for 5-10 minutes until lightly browned and crispy and then set aside to cool completely.

3. Stuff the chicken with the prunes, apples and peanuts. Place the chicken into the Instant Pot. Pour some sunflower oil and close the lid to cook on a MEDIUM pressure for 50 minutes.

4. Quick-release the pressure.

5. Portion the chicken into three plates and dollop each plate with the greenery. Remember that this dish should be served warm. Serve the chicken with the salad.

Nutrition (Per Serving):

Calories: 242; Fat: 45g; Carbohydrates: 174g; Protein: 32g

Paleo Chicken Thighs with Basil

Serving: 4

Prep Time: 10 minutes

Cook Time: 45 minutes

Ingredients:

- 8 chicken thighs
- 4 oranges, peeled and diced
- 5 tablespoons herbs
- 2 tablespoons soy sauce
- 4 tablespoons dry basil
- 5 garlic cloves, minced
- 4 tablespoons olive oil
- Salt as needed
- 1 cup of freshly squeezed orange juice
- ½ tablespoon of corn starch
- ½ cup of water

How to Prepare:

1. Marinate the chicken thighs in the salt, soy sauce, dry basil, minced garlic, orange juice and herbs for at least few hours unrefrigerated at room temperature or place in the fridge overnight. Add the marinated chicken thighs and all the listed ingredients to your Instant Pot.

2. Close the lid and set the timer to 45 minutes and cook the chicken on MEAT/STEW mode.

3. Release the pressure naturally over 10 minutes.

4. Serve and enjoy!

Nutrition (Per Serving):

Calories: 326; Fat: 73g; Carbohydrates: 245g; Protein: 56g

Chicken Meatballs with Champignons

Serving: 4

Prep Time: 10 minutes

Cooking Time: 30 minutes

Ingredients:

- 40 oz ground chicken
- 15 oz champignons, diced
- 4 tablespoons walnuts
- 1 tablespoon sesame seeds oil
- ¼ teaspoon each pepper and salt
- 5 tablespoons lemon juice
- 2 teaspoons nutmeg
- 2 teaspoons dried basil

How to Prepare:

1. Preheat the oven to 250°-270° Fahrenheit and roast the walnuts in the oven for 5-10 minutes until lightly browned and crispy and then set aside to cool completely. Grind the nuts.
2. In the Instant Pot, heat the oil and sauté the champignons for 10 minutes. Combine the meat with the champignons, spices and nuts and form the chicken meatballs.
3. Place the chicken meatballs into the Instant Pot and pour some sesame seeds oil. Close the lid to cook on a HIGH pressure for 30 minutes.
4. Quick-release the pressure.
5. Season with the salt and pepper.
6. Portion the chicken meatballs into four plates and dollop each plate with the lemon juice. Remember that this dish should be served warm.

Nutrition (Per Serving):

Calories: 187; Fat: 36g; Carbohydrates: 159g; Protein: 32g

Paleo Chicken with Prunes

Serving: 4

Prep Time: 10 minutes

Cooking Time: 50 minutes

Ingredients:

- 1 chicken
- 2 cups of prunes
- 5 sour apples, diced
- 3 tablespoons sunflower oil
- 1 teaspoon each pepper and salt
- 5 garlic cloves, minced
- 1 bunch of greenery, chopped

How to Prepare:

1. Toss the chicken carcass in salt, pepper and garlic and marinate for few hours.

2. Stuff the chicken with the prunes and apples. Place the chicken into the Instant Pot. Pour some sunflower oil and close the lid to cook on a MEDIUM pressure for 50 minutes.

3. Quick-release the pressure.

4. Portion the chicken into four plates. Remember that this dish should be served warm.

Nutrition (Per Serving):

Calories: 288; Fat: 45g; Carbohydrates: 192g; Protein: 39g

Zucchini Spaghetti with Chicken

Serving: 4

Prep Time: 10 minutes

Cooking Time: 45 minutes

Ingredients:

- 25 oz chicken, diced
- 2 medium zucchinis, spiralized
- 1 cup of walnuts
- 3 tablespoons soy sauce
- 1 tablespoon dry basil
- 4 garlic cloves, minced
- 5 tablespoons Olive oil
- 2 tablespoons corn starch
- 1 cup of water
- 2 teaspoons salt
- black pepper, to taste
- fresh parsley

How to Prepare:

1. Preheat the oven to 250°-270°Fahrenheit and roast the walnuts in the oven for 10 minutes until lightly browned and crispy and then set aside to cool completely. Then grind the walnuts using a food processor or blender.

2. Add in all the listed ingredients to your Pot and close the lid to cook on MEAT/STEW mode. Remember to set the timer to 45 minutes.

3. Release the pressure over 10 minutes.

4. Serve the zucchini spaghetti with the fresh parsley and enjoy!

Nutrition (Per Serving):

Calories: 241; Fat: 43g; Carbohydrates: 181g; Protein: 37g

Goose with Pumpkin Puree

Serving: 5

Prep Time: 15 minute

Cooking Time: 55 minutes

Ingredients:

- 5 lb goose, cubed
- 1 lb pumpkin, cubed
- 20 oz tomatoes, cubed
- 5 onions, peeled and chopped
- 1 cup of water
- Salt and pepper to taste

How to Prepare:

1. Add the water to your Instant Pot and place the cubed goose, pumpkin, tomatoes and onions. Add salt and pepper. Close the lid and cook on a MEDIUM pressure for 55 minutes.

2. Quick-release the pressure and let the pumpkin to cool.

3. Mash the pumpkin, tomatoes and onions using the potato masher and season with the salt and pepper to taste.

4. Portion the goose with the pumpkin puree into the five bowls or mugs. Remember that this dish should be served warm.

Nutrition (Per Serving):

Calories: 324; Fat: 48g; Carbohydrates: 262g; Protein: 35g

Chicken Wings in Sauce

Serving: 5

Prep Time: 15 minute

Cooking Time: 55 minutes

Ingredients:

- 4 lb chicken wings
- 1 packet garlic powder
- 1 bottle Buffalo wing sauce
- 5 tablespoons sunflower oil
- Salt and pepper to taste

How to Prepare:

1. In a bowl, toss the chicken wings in the garlic powder, salt and pepper. Then set the wings aside to marinate for at least 2 hours unrefrigerated at room temperature.

2. Heat the Instant Pot and pour some oil. Place the chicken wings into the Pot. Pour some Buffalo wing sauce. Close the lid and cook on a MEDIUM pressure for 35 minutes.

3. Quick-release the pressure.

4. Portion the chicken wings into five plates and dollop each plate with the remaining Buffalo sauce. Remember that this dish should be served warm.

Nutrition (Per Serving):

Calories: 328; Fat: 45g; Carbohydrates: 268g; Protein: 37g

Chicken with Pumpkin and Tomatoes

Serving: 5

Prep Time: 15 minute

Cooking Time: 45 minutes

Ingredients:

- 5 chicken thighs
- 3 lb small-sized pumpkin, seeded and diced
- 20 oz tomatoes, diced
- 4 tablespoons, garlic powder
- 5 onions, peeled and chopped
- 1 cup of water
- Salt and pepper to taste
- 1 bunch of greenery

How to Prepare:

1. Marinate the chicken thighs in garlic powder for 5 hours.

2. Add the water to your Instant Pot and place the chicken, tomatoes and diced pumpkin. Close the lid to cook on a MEDIUM pressure for 45 minutes.

3. Quick-release the pressure.

4. Portion the chicken and pumpkin into five plates and dollop each plate with the greenery. Remember that this dish should be served warm.

Nutrition (Per Serving):

Calories: 186; Fat: 44g; Carbohydrates: 152g; Protein: 34g

Spicy Paleo Chicken Hearts Bouillon

Serving: 4

Prep Time: 10 minutes

Cooking Time: 35 minutes

Ingredients:

- 25 chicken hearts
- 1 bunch of parsley, chopped
- 1 bunch of chives, chopped
- 2 bay leaves
- 2 teaspoons chili pepper powder
- 2 medium onions, chopped
- 1 garlic, smashed
- salt and pepper as needed
- 2 teaspoons cilantro for garnish
- 8 cups of water

How to Prepare:

1. Pour the water and set the Instant Pot to sauté mode.
2. Add the onions and chili pepper powder and sauté for 5 minutes until clear and caramelized.
3. Add in the chicken hearts, bay leaves, cilantro, garlic and season with the salt and pepper.
4. Close the lid and cook on a MEDIUM pressure for 30 minutes.
5. Release the pressure over 10 minutes.
6. Portion the soup into four bowls or mugs and dollop each bowl with the chopped parsley and chives. Remember that this dish should be served warm.

Nutrition (Per Serving):

Calories: 232; Fat: 55g; Carbohydrates: 181g; Protein: 41g

French Chicken Livers with Tomatoes

Serving: 4

Prep Time: 10 minutes

Cooking Time: 30 minutes

Ingredients:

- 20 oz chicken livers
- 2 onions, peeled and chopped
- 2 tablespoons white flour
- 4 tablespoons coconut oil
- 5 tomatoes, diced
- 2 tablespoons garlic powder
- ¼ teaspoon each pepper and salt
- 1 bunch of greenery, chopped

How to Prepare:

1. Toss the chicken livers in salt, pepper, garlic powder and white flour.

2. Heat the coconut oil in the Instant Pot and select the sauté mode to heat the oil. Spoon the onions and sauté for 10 minutes to clear and caramelized.

3. Place the chicken livers and tomatoes into the Instant Pot. Close the lid and cook on a MEDIUM pressure for 30 minutes.

4. Quick-release the pressure and open the lid.

5. Portion the chicken livers into four plates and dollop each plate with the greenery. Remember that this dish should be served warm. Serve the chicken livers with the salad.

Nutrition (Per Serving):

Calories: 267; Fat: 48g; Carbohydrates: 215g; Protein: 38g

Chicken Breast with Pineapple Rings

Serving: 4

Prep Time: 10 minutes

Cooking Time: 30 minutes

Ingredients:

- 3 lb chicken breast, sliced
- 1 can pineapple rings
- 4 tablespoons coconut oil
- 2 tablespoons garlic powder
- 1 teaspoon chili powder
- ¼ teaspoon each pepper and salt
- 2 oz Vegan cheese, grated

How to Prepare:

1. Toss the chicken breast in salt, pepper, garlic powder and chili powder.
2. Heat the coconut oil in the Instant Pot and select the sauté mode to heat the oil.
3. Place the chicken breast slices into the Instant Pot. Close the lid and cook on a MEDIUM pressure for 30 minutes.
4. Quick-release the pressure and open the lid. Dollop each chicken slice with the pineapple ring and then spoon the grated Vegan cheese on top. Close the lid for 10 minutes to melt the cheese.
5. Portion the chicken breast into four plates. Remember that this dish should be served warm. Serve the chicken breast with the vegetables.

Nutrition (Per Serving):

Calories: 274; Fat: 34g; Carbohydrates: 180g; Protein: 32g

Paleo Creamy Chicken Soup

Serving: 5

Prep Time: 15 minutes

Cooking Time: 60 minutes

Ingredients:

- 5 chicken boneless thighs, cubed
- 25 oz smoked bacon, cubed
- 4 tablespoons extra virgin olive oil
- 5 tablespoons vegan cream cheese
- 2 yellow onions, chopped
- 1 teaspoon dried thyme
- 3 tablespoons garlic powder
- 3 garlic cloves, chopped
- 2 tablespoons white flour
- 5 oz celery, diced
- 10 oz champignons, diced
- 1 tablespoon curry powder
- 6 cups of water
- 2 cups of vegetable broth
- fresh greenery, chopped

- salt and pepper

How to Prepare:

1. In a bowl, combine the dried thyme, curry powder, garlic powder, salt and pepper. Toss the chicken thighs in spices. Marinate the chicken in the Ziploc storage bag for 4 hours in the refrigerator.
2. Add some oil to the Instant Pot and set it to the sauté mode.
3. Add in the onions and garlic and sauté for 15 minutes until clear and caramelized.
4. Add the vegetable broth and mix well.
5. Sauté for 5 minutes.
6. Add in the white flour, celery, champignons, vegan cream cheese, smoked bacon and chicken. Pour the water and close the lid.
7. Cook on a MEDIUM pressure for 40 minutes.
8. Release the pressure naturally.
9. Add in the chopped greenery and mix well.
10. Portion the chicken soup into the five bowls or mugs. Remember that this dish should be served warm.

Nutrition (Per Serving):

Calories: 243; Fat: 42g; Carbohydrates: 212g; Protein: 37g

Chicken Breast with Zucchini

Serving: 4

Prep Time: 15 minutes

Cook Time: 60 minutes

Ingredients:

- 3 lb ground chicken breast
- 4 medium-sized zucchinis, halved
- 2 cups of water
- 20 oz Vegan cheese, grated
- 1 cup of marinated black olives, pitted and chopped
- 5-7 garlic cloves, sliced
- 5 tablespoons Olive oil
- 1 teaspoon salt
- 5 fresh basil leaves
- 1 teaspoon chili pepper
- 1 teaspoon dry basil

How to Prepare:

1. Halve the zucchinis and scoop out the seeds.

2. Meanwhile, in a skillet or wok, heat the Olive oil and stew the garlic for 5 minutes until clear. Then add in the ground chicken to fry for 15 minutes until golden brown. Add some salt, basil and chili pepper.
3. Spoon the ground chicken into the zucchini halves. Add in the water to the Instant Pot and place a trivet on top.
4. Place the zucchini halves on the trivet. The flesh side facing up. Close the lid and cook on a HIGH pressure for 35 minutes.
5. Once the cooking is done, allow the pressure to release naturally.
6. In a bowl, combine the cheese and all the remaining ingredients.
7. Add a spoonful of vegan cheese mixture into each zucchini half and stew for 5 minutes to melt the cheese.
8. Portion the zucchini into four plates and dollop each plate with the basil. Remember that this dish should be served warm.

Nutrition (Per Serving):

Calories: 232; Fat: 38g; Carbohydrates: 180g; Protein: 35g

Paleo Soup with Chicken Sausages

Serving: 5

Prep Time: 10 minutes

Cook Time: 50 minutes

Ingredients:

- 40 oz chicken or turkey sausages, cubed
- 20 oz fresh kale
- 6 cups of water
- 2 onions, peeled and chopped
- 1 cup of coconut milk
- 4 yellow bell peppers, cut into long pieces
- 3 tablespoons white flour
- 4 garlic cloves, chopped
- 4 tablespoons Olive oil
- 1 teaspoon turmeric
- 1 teaspoon dried fennel
- 2 teaspoons dried basil
- Salt and pepper
- 1 tablespoon cayenne pepper powder

How to Prepare:

1. Pour the olive oil into the Instant Pot. Set the Instant Pot to the sauté mode and add in the onions and bell peppers. Sauté for 10 minutes until clear and caramelized.
2. Mix in the garlic and turmeric and simmer for 5 minutes.
3. Add in the chicken sausages, fresh kale, coconut milk, white flour, turmeric, dried fennel, basil, salt, pepper, cayenne pepper powder.
4. Pour the water and close the lid to cook on a HIGH pressure for 35 minutes. Release the pressure naturally.
5. Mix well and portion the soup into the five bowls. Remember that this dish should be served warm.

Nutrition (Per Serving):

Calories: 196; Fat: 48g; Carbohydrates: 154g; Protein: 39g

Paleo Chicken Meatballs

Serving: 4

Prep Time: 10 minutes

Cooking Time: 30 minutes

Ingredients:

- 3 lb chicken, ground
- 1 cup of corn
- 1 tablespoon sunflower oil
- ¼ teaspoon each pepper and salt
- 5 tablespoons lemon juice

How to Prepare:

1. Combine the chicken meat with the spices and form the chicken meatballs.
2. Place the chicken meatballs into the Instant Pot and pour some sunflower oil. Close the lid to cook on a HIGH pressure for 30 minutes.
3. Quick-release the pressure.
4. Season with the salt and pepper.

5. Portion the paleo chicken meatballs into four plates and dollop each plate with the lemon juice. Remember that this dish should be served warm.

Nutrition (Per Serving):

Calories: 232; Fat: 38g; Carbohydrates: 189g; Protein: 33g

Turkey with Pumpkin with Champignons

Serving: 3

Prep Time: 15 minute

Cooking Time: 60 minutes

Ingredients:

- 3 lb turkey, diced
- 2 lb small-sized pumpkin, diced
- 20 oz champignons
- 5 onions, peeled and chopped
- 1 red bell pepper, chopped
- 5 tablespoons coconut oil
- Salt and pepper to taste
- 1 bunch of greenery, chopped

How to Prepare:

1. In the Instant Pot, heat the coconut oil. Select the sauté mode. Spoon the onions and sauté for around 10 minutes until clear and golden. Then chop the champignons and spoon into the Instant Pot. Sauté for 10 minutes until brown. Add in the turkey and bell pepper. Sauté for 10 minutes. Mix the turkey and vegetables well and sprinkle some salt and pepper.

2. Pour the water to your Instant Pot and place the diced pumpkin. Close the lid to cook on a HIGH pressure for 30 minutes.

3. Quick-release the pressure and let the turkey and vegetables to cool.

4. Season with the salt and pepper to taste.

5. Portion the turkey into three bowls or mugs and dollop each bowl with the chopped greenery. Remember that this dish should be served warm. Serve the turkey with the vegetables.

Nutrition (Per Serving):

Calories: 258; Fat: 34g; Carbohydrates: 169g; Protein: 38g

Paleo Chicken and Broccoli Soup

Serving: 4

Prep Time: 15 minutes

Cooking Time: 50 minutes

Ingredients:

- 3 lb chicken, diced
- 2 medium broccolis
- ½ of yellow onion, chopped
- 2 carrots, peeled and diced
- 3 garlic cloves, minced
- 10 oz fresh kale, minced
- 1 tablespoon of curry powder
- 1 teaspoon of cayenne pepper
- 6 cups of water
- 2 cups of vegetable broth
- fresh greenery, chopped
- 4 tablespoons extra virgin olive oil

How to Prepare:

1. Add some oil to the Instant Pot and set it to the sauté mode.

2. Add in the onions and garlic and sauté for 15 minutes until clear and caramelized.
3. Add the vegetable broth, cayenne and curry powder, mix well.
4. Sauté for 5 minutes.
5. Add all the remaining ingredients (except kale) and close the lid.
6. Cook on a MEDIUM pressure for 40 minutes.
7. Release the pressure naturally.
8. Add in the chopped up kale and mix well.
9. Portion the chicken and broccoli soup into four bowls or mugs and dollop each bowl with the fresh greenery. Remember that this dish should be served warm.

Nutrition (Per Serving):

Calories: 232; Fat: 39g; Carbohydrates: 210g; Protein: 36g

Instant Pot Paleo Omelet Recipes

Omelet with Spinach, Basil and Sausages

Serving: 4

Prep Time: 15 minutes

Cooking Time: 30 minutes

Ingredients:

- 6 eggs
- 15 oz spinach, chopped
- 4 medium chicken sausages, cubed
- 2 medium onions, chopped
- 3 tablespoon Olive oil
- 1/2 cup of water
- 2 tablespoons oil or baking spray
- 1 teaspoon basil
- salt, to taste
- pepper, to taste

How to Prepare:

1. Grease the Pot with the oil or baking spray and add in the onions.
2. In a bowl, beat the eggs and the salt using an electric hand mixer until there is a smooth and creamy consistency and homogenous mass. Add in some basil.
3. Combine all the ingredients with the chicken sausages, croutons and eggs and pour the eggs mixture into the Instant Pot.
4. Add some water to your pot and close the lid.
5. Cook on a LOW pressure for 15 minutes and then release the pressure naturally.
6. Sprinkle the salt and pepper and you are free to serve the omelet with the sausages and spinach in separate dishes with the coffee. Remember that this dish should be served warm.

Nutrition (Per Serving)

Calories: 179; Fat: 34g; Carbohydrates: 129g; Protein: 32g

Omelet with Avocado and Chives

Serving: 4

Prep Time: 15 minutes

Cooking Time: 30 minutes

Ingredients:

- 6 eggs
- 1 avocado, sliced
- 3 tablespoon Olive oil
- 1/2 cup of water
- 2 teaspoons dry onions
- 2 tablespoons oil or baking spray
- 1 teaspoon herbs
- salt, to taste
- pepper, to taste
- 1 bunch of chives, chopped

How to Prepare:

1. Grease the Pot with the oil or baking spray and add in the tomatoes.
2. In a bowl, beat the eggs and the salt using an electric hand mixer until there is a smooth and creamy consistency and homogenous mass.
3. Combine all the ingredients (except the avocado) with the eggs and pour the eggs mixture into the Pot. Close the lid.
4. Cook on a LOW pressure for 15 minutes and then release the pressure naturally.
5. Sprinkle the salt and pepper and you are free to serve the eggs with the avocados in separate dishes. Remember that this dish should be served warm.

Nutrition (Per Serving)

Calories: 260; Fat: 33g; Carbohydrates: 175g; Protein: 26g

Paleo Omelet with Smoked Ham

Serving: 2

Prep Time: 15 minutes

Cooking Time: 35 minutes

Ingredients:

- 5 eggs
- 12 oz smoked ham, cubed
- 4 tablespoon extra-virgin olive oil
- 4 teaspoons mayonnaise
- 10 garlic cloves, minced
- 2 medium onions, peeled and chopped
- 4 tablespoons oil butter
- 1 bunch of chives, chopped
- salt, to taste
- pepper, to taste

How to Prepare:

1. In a skillet, heat the oil and fry the cubed ham for 10 minutes until golden brown and crispy. Then add in the onions and fry for 10 minutes until caramelized.
2. In a bowl, combine the eggs with the mayonnaise, oil and the salt and then beat the ingredients using an electric hand mixer until there is a smooth and creamy consistency and homogenous mass.
3. Combine all the ingredients with the eggs and pour the mixture into the Instant Pot. Close the lid.
4. Cook on a LOW pressure for 15 minutes and then release the pressure naturally.
5. Sprinkle the salt and pepper and you are free to serve the omelet with the ham in separate plates. Sprinkle some chopped chives on top. Remember that this dish should be served warm.

Nutrition (Per Serving)

Calories: 224; Fat: 25g; Carbohydrates: 73g; Protein: 24g

Paleo Omelet with Bacon and Bell Peppers

Serving: 4

Prep Time: 10 minutes

Cooking Time: 35 minutes

Ingredients:

- 6 eggs
- 6 bacon slices
- 10 oz spinach, chopped
- 3 red bell peppers, chopped
- 2 teaspoons dry onions
- 4 tablespoons Olive oil or baking spray
- 1 teaspoon herbs
- salt, to taste
- pepper, to taste
- 1 bunch of chives

How to Prepare:

1. Grease the Instant Pot with the Olive oil.
2. In the Instant Pot, heat 2 tablespoons Olive oil and sauté the bacon slices on a low heat for 10 minutes until golden brown and crispy. Then spoon the bell peppers and simmer for 10 minutes.
3. In a bowl, beat the eggs with the cream and salt using an electric hand mixer until there is a smooth and creamy consistency and homogenous mass.
4. Pour the eggs mixture into the Instant Pot. Mix in the spinach, onions, herbs, salt, pepper and chives.
5. Cook on a MEDIUM pressure for 10-15 minutes and then release the pressure naturally.
6. Sprinkle the salt and pepper. Portion the omelet with the bacon into three plates or bowls.

Nutrition (Per Serving)

Calories: 174; Fat: 25g; Carbohydrates: 57g; Protein: 25g

Fish Omelet with Parsley

Serving: 3

Prep Time: 10 minutes

Cooking Time: 25 minutes

Ingredients:

- 6 eggs
- 20 oz smoked salmon, diced
- a drizzle of extra virgin olive oil
- 2 medium yellow onions, peeled and chopped
- salt and black pepper, to taste
- 1 bunch of parsley, chopped

How to Prepare:

1. Beat the eggs using an electric hand mixer until there is a creamy consistency and homogenous mass.
2. Set the Instant Pot to sauté mode. Heat the olive oil and sauté the chopped yellow onion for 5-10 minutes until clear and caramelized.
3. In a bowl, mix the eggs with the salt, pepper, salmon and onions and whisk them well.

4. Slightly pour the egg mixture into the Instant Pot. Stir the eggs mixture well.
5. Press the Air Crisp mode and cook the eggs at 250° Fahrenheit for 15 minutes.
6. Portion the omelet into plates and dollop each plate with the lemon juice. Serve the salmon omelet with the tea and toasts.

Nutrition (Per Serving):

Calories: 175; Fat: 36g; Carbohydrates: 105g; Protein: 32g

Salmon Omelet with Champignons and Sausages

Serving: 4

Prep Time: 10 minutes

Cooking Time: 40 minutes

Ingredients:

- 8 eggs
- 25 oz smoked salmon, sliced
- 4 breakfast sausages, diced
- 20 oz champignons, diced
- 2 tablespoons olive oil
- 2 medium onions, peeled and chopped
- salt and black pepper, to taste
- 1 bunch of parsley

How to Prepare:

1. Whisk the eggs using an electric hand mixer until there is a creamy consistency and homogenous mass.
2. In the Instant Pot, heat the olive oil and sauté the champignons for 10 minutes until golden brown and crispy. Then add in the chopped onions and diced sausages and sauté for 10 minutes until clear and caramelized.
3. In the Instant Pot, combine the eggs mixture with the salt, pepper, champignons, salmon, sausages and onions.
4. Set the Pot on Air Crisp mode and cook the eggs at 250° Fahrenheit for 20 minutes.
5. Portion the salmon omelet into the plates or bowls and dollop each bowl with the chopped parsley. Remember that this dish should be served warm. Serve the salmon omelet with the coffee and cucumbers.

Nutrition (Per Serving):

Calories: 175; Fat: 35g; Carbohydrates: 74g; Protein: 30g

Tomatoes Omelet with Cashews

Serving: 3

Prep Time: 15 minutes

Cooking Time: 20 minutes

Ingredients:

- 6 eggs
- 2 cups of cashews
- 3 cups of cherry tomatoes, halved
- 3 tablespoon Olive oil
- salt, to taste
- pepper, to taste

How to Prepare:

1. In a skillet, fry the cherry tomatoes for 5-10 minutes.
2. In a bowl, beat the eggs with the salt using an electric hand mixer until there is a smooth and creamy consistency and homogenous mass.
3. Heat the Instant Pot and pour all the ingredients into the Pot.
4. Then close the lid.

5. Cook on a LOW pressure for 20 minutes and then release the pressure naturally.
6. Serve the omelet in separate plates with the coffee. Remember that this dish should be served warm.

<u>Nutrition (Per Serving)</u>

Calories: 124; Fat: 28g; Carbohydrates: 92g; Protein: 24g

Omelet with Turkey Sausages

Serving: 4

Prep Time: 15 minutes

Cooking Time: 35 minutes

Ingredients:

- 8 eggs
- 25 oz turkey sausages, cubed
- 5 garlic cloves, minced
- 3 tablespoon Olive oil
- 1 teaspoon herbs
- 10 oz celery, diced
- salt, to taste
- pepper, to taste

How to Prepare:

1. In a skillet or wok, heat the oil and fry the sausages for 10 minutes until crispy and golden brown. Add in the celery and stew for 10 minutes.
2. Grease the Instant Pot with the oil or baking spray.
3. In a bowl, beat the eggs with the salt using an electric hand mixer until there is a smooth and creamy consistency and homogenous mass. Mix in the herbs.
4. Combine all the ingredients with the sausages and eggs mixture. Pour into the Instant Pot and close the lid.
5. Cook on a LOW pressure for 15 minutes and then release the pressure naturally.
6. Sprinkle the salt and pepper to taste and you are free to serve the omelet in separate dishes. Remember that this dish should be served warm.

Nutrition (Per Serving)

Calories: 152; Fat: 28g; Carbohydrates: 121g; Protein: 24g

Scrambled Eggs with Sausages and Peanuts

Serving: 4

Prep Time: 15 minutes

Cooking Time: 50 minutes

Ingredients:

- 5 eggs
- 5 beef sausages, cubed
- 1 cup of peanuts
- 3 tablespoon Olive oil
- 2 tablespoons oil or baking spray
- 1 teaspoon herbs
- salt, to taste
- pepper, to taste

How to Prepare:

1. Preheat the oven to 250°-270°Fahrenheit and roast the peanuts in the oven for 10 minutes until lightly browned and crispy and then set aside to cool completely. Then grind the peanuts using a food processor or blender.
2. Grease the Pot with the oil or baking spray. In a skillet, heat the oil and fry the beef sausages for 5 or 10 minutes.
3. In a bowl, beat the eggs and the salt using an electric hand mixer until there is a smooth and creamy consistency and homogenous mass.
4. Combine all the ingredients with the peanuts and beef sausages and pour the eggs mixture into the Instant Pot. Then close the lid and cook on a LOW pressure for 15 minutes. Release the pressure naturally.
5. Sprinkle the salt and pepper to taste and you are free to serve the scrambled eggs in separate dishes with the bread.

Nutrition (Per Serving)

Calories: 164; Fat: 24g; Carbohydrates: 114g; Protein: 21g

Instant Pot Paleo Fish Recipes

Spicy Paleo Shrimps

Serving: 3

Prep Time: 10 minutes

Cooking Time: 40 minutes

Ingredients:

- 35 oz shrimps
- 1 cup of lemon juice
- 3 cups of water
- 2 tablespoons olive oil
- ½ teaspoon salt and pepper
- 2 medium onions, chopped
- 1 teaspoon nutmeg
- 1 teaspoon chili powder
- 5 cloves minced garlic
- 1 bunch of greenery, chopped
- 1 tablespoon lemon juice

How to Prepare:

1. In a bowl, combine the nutmeg, chili, salt, garlic and black pepper. Season the shrimps with the spices mix. Set the shrimps aside to marinate for at least few hours unrefrigerated at room temperature or place in the fridge for overnight.

2. In the Instant Pot, heat the oil and sauté the shrimps for around 10 minutes until golden brown. Mix in the onions and stew for 10 minutes until clear and caramelized with the lid closed.

3. Combine the shrimps and all the remaining ingredients and add them to the Instant Pot. Pour some water.

4. Close the lid and cook on a MEDIUM pressure for 20 minutes.

5. Release the pressure naturally over 10 minutes.

6. Portion the shrimps into three bowls or mugs and dollop each bowl with the chopped greenery. Sprinkle some lemon juice. Serve the shrimps with the beer.

Nutrition (Per Serving)

Calories: 165; Fat: 26g; Carbohydrates: 59g; Protein: 25g

Bell Peppers with Fish and Pumpkin

Serving: 3

Prep Time: 5 minutes

Cook Time: 35 minutes

Ingredients:

- 25 oz ground fish
- 4 yellow bell peppers, cut into long pieces
- 1 cup of pumpkin, peeled and cubed
- 1 cup of raisins
- 3 tablespoons white flour
- ½ teaspoon cumin seeds
- 4 garlic cloves, chopped
- 4 tablespoons pumpkin seeds oil
- Cilantro for garnish
- 1 teaspoon turmeric
- ½ a teaspoon cayenne pepper
- 2 teaspoons coriander
- 4 tablespoons lemon juice

How to Prepare:

1. Wash and soak the raisins in the warm water for around 20 minutes and then chop them.
2. Set the Instant Pot to the sauté mode and add in the pumpkin seeds oil, then heat up the oil.
3. Mix in the garlic and cumin and simmer for 5 minutes until clear and caramelized.
4. Stir in the ground fish, bell peppers, spices, flour, and pumpkin. Mix in all the remaining ingredients.
5. Pour some water and close the lid to cook on a HIGH pressure for 35 minutes.
6. Release the pressure naturally and add the lemon juice.
7. Mix well and portion the fish into three plates and sprinkle each plate with the cilantro. Remember that this dish should be served warm. Serve the chicken and vegetables with the tomato and onion salad.

Nutrition (Per Serving):

Calories: 189; Fat: 37g; Carbohydrates: 115g; Protein: 29g

Paleo Pike with Onions and Champignons

Serving: 3

Prep Time: 10 minutes

Cooking Time: 50 minutes

Ingredients:

- 1 pike, cut into inch strips
- 15 oz champignons, sliced
- 1 cup of water
- 3 tablespoons flour
- 4 medium onions, peeled and chopped
- 5 cloves garlic, minced
- 2 tablespoons basil
- salt and pepper, to taste

How to Prepare:

1. In the Instant Pot, heat the oil and sauté the onions for 10 minutes until clear and caramelized. Add in the champignons and sauté for 10 minutes.

2. Toss the pike in the minced garlic, basil, salt and pepper. Marinate for around 2 hours. Then toss the fish in the flour. Pour some water and add the onions and fish into the Instant Pot. Cook the fish strips on a LOW pressure for 30 minutes.

3. Release the pressure naturally over 10 minutes.

4. Portion the pike into three plates. Sprinkle with the lime juice. Remember that this dish should be served warm.

Nutrition (Per Serving)

Calories: 261; Fat: 40g; Carbohydrates: 209g; Protein: 30g

Paleo Salmon with Portobello Mushrooms

Serving: 4

Prep Time: 10 minutes

Cooking Time: 50 minutes

Ingredients:

- 20 oz salmon fillet, cut into stripes
- 15 oz Portobello mushrooms, sliced
- 3 tablespoons flour
- 2 eggs
- 4 medium onions, peeled and chopped
- 5 cloves garlic, minced
- 2 tablespoons basil
- salt and pepper, to taste
- 2 tablespoons lime juice

How to Prepare:

1. In the Instant Pot, heat the oil and sauté the onions for 10 minutes until clear and caramelized. Add in the Portobello mushrooms and sauté for 10 minutes.

2. In a bowl, whisk the eggs until creamy consistency.

3. Toss the salmon in the minced garlic, basil, salt and pepper. Marinate for around 2 hours. Then toss the fish in the eggs and flour. Add the salmon into the Instant Pot. Cook the fish strips on a LOW pressure for 30 minutes.

4. Release the pressure naturally over 10 minutes.

5. Portion the salmon into four plates. Sprinkle with the lime juice. Remember that this dish should be served warm.

Nutrition (Per Serving)

Calories: 251; Fat: 42g; Carbohydrates: 212g; Protein: 32g

Paleo Fish Soup

Serving: 5

Prep Time: 15 minutes

Cooking Time: 50 minutes

Ingredients:

- 10 medium common roaches (Rutilus rutilus)
- 2 teaspoons chili pepper powder
- 1 medium onion, chopped
- 5 garlic cloves, smashed
- salt and pepper, to taste
- 1 cup of fish stock
- 5 cups of water
- ¼ cup of cilantro for garnish
- 1 teaspoon rosemary
- 3 bay leaves
- 1 teaspoon basil
- 1 bunch of parsley, chopped
- 1 bunch of dill, chopped

How to Prepare:

1. Set your Instant Pot to sauté mode and add some sunflower oil.
2. Add the chili pepper powder and sauté for 5 minutes.
3. Add the onion, 2 tablespoons cilantro, garlic and season with the salt and pepper.
4. Sauté for 5 minutes and add the fish stock.
5. Season the fish with the rosemary and salt and marinate for at least few hours unrefrigerated at room temperature.
6. In the Instant Pot, combine the chili pepper powder, bay leaves, basil, parsley and dill. Add the fish and pour the water.
7. Close the lid and cook on a LOW pressure for 40 minutes.
8. Release the pressure over 10 minutes.
9. Portion the soup into five bowls or mugs and dollop each bowl with the chopped dill. Remember that this dish should be served warm.

Nutrition (Per Serving):

Calories: 248; Fat: 48g; Carbohydrates: 162g; Protein: 38g

Paleo Salmon Rolls with Zucchini

Serving: 4

Prep Time: 10 minutes

Cooking Time: 55 minutes

Ingredients:

- 35 oz salmon fillet, sliced
- 10 oz zucchini, spiralized
- 1 cup of raisins
- 1 cup of onions, peeled and chopped
- 2 cups of walnuts
- 3 tablespoons sunflower oil
- 4 garlic cloves, minced
- Salt, to taste

How to Prepare:

1. Preheat the oven to 240°- 250° Fahrenheit and roast the walnuts in the oven for 10 minutes until lightly browned and crispy and then set aside to cool completely. Grind the walnuts using a food processor or blender.

2. In the Instant Pot, heat the sunflower oil and simmer the zucchini and onions for 10-15 minutes until clear and caramelized. Add the walnuts, raisins, garlic and some salt. Mix well.

3. Spoon the filling over the salmon slices. Roll the salmon slices tightly encasing the filling inside. Then tie the salmon rolls firmly with the kitchen twine. Add them to your instant pot and close the lid to cook on a MEDIUM pressure for 25 minutes.

4. Portion the salmon roulades into four plates. Remember that this dish should be served warm.

Nutrition (Per Serving):

Calories: 241; Fat: 35g; Carbohydrates: 178g; Protein: 27g

Paleo Salmon Balls with Tomato Sauce

Serving: 2

Prep Time: 10 minutes

Cooking Time: 30 minutes

Ingredients:

- 2 lb salmon, ground
- 2 tablespoons coconut oil
- 2 tablespoons garlic powder
- 2 tablespoons onion powder
- 1 tablespoon smoked paprika
- ¼ teaspoon each pepper and salt
- 1 cup of tomato sauce

How to Prepare:

1. Mix together garlic powder, onion powder, smoked paprika, salt and pepper.
2. Combine the ground salmon with this mix.
3. Pour some coconut oil into the Instant Pot. Select the sauté mode and heat the oil in the Instant Pot.

4. Place the salmon balls into the Instant Pot. Close the lid and cook until brown on both sides. Cook on a MEDIUM pressure for 30 minutes.

5. Quick-release the pressure and open the lid.

6. Portion the fish balls into two plates and dollop each plate with the greenery. Remember that this dish should be served warm. Serve the fish balls with the salad.

Nutrition (Per Serving):

Calories: 225; Fat: 35g; Carbohydrates: 176g; Protein: 31g

Paleo Shrimps Bouillon with Pineapple

Serving: 2

Prep Time: 10 minutes

Cooking Time: 60 minutes

Ingredients:

- 40 oz medium shrimps
- 1 chili pepper
- 2 cups of pineapple cubes
- 3 tablespoons frozen vegetable mix
- 2 carrots, peeled and diced
- 5 cups of water
- 3 teaspoons basil, dried and crushed
- 1/8 teaspoon oregano, crushed
- ½ medium onion, chopped
- 4 garlic cloves, minced
- sea salt and black pepper, to taste

How to Prepare:

1. Add all the ingredients to the Instant Pot and mix well.
2. Close the lid and select the slow mode to cook for 60 minutes.

3. Keep the pressure and then release the handle to the Venting position.

4. Once cooked, stir the bouillon well.

5. Portion the bouillon into two bowls or mugs. Remember that this dish should be served warm.

Nutrition (Per Serving):

Calories: 267; Fat: 54g; Carbohydrates: 172g; Protein: 40g

Shrimps Soup with Parsley

Serving: 3

Prep Time: 10 minutes

Cooking Time: 35 minutes

Ingredients:

- 40 oz of shrimps, cleaned and deveined
- 4 tablespoon sunflower oil
- 1 bunch of parsley, chopped
- 2 bay leaves
- 2 teaspoons chili pepper powder
- 1 medium onion, thinly sliced
- 1 green bell pepper, thinly sliced
- 2 cloves garlic, smashed
- salt and pepper as needed
- 1 cup fish stock
- 12 littleneck clams
- ¼ cup cilantro for garnish

How to Prepare:

1. Set your Instant Pot to sauté mode and add some sunflower oil.

2. Add the bay leaves and chili pepper powder and sauté for 5 minutes.
3. Add in the onion, bell pepper, 2 tablespoons of cilantro, garlic and season with the salt and pepper.
4. Stir for a few minutes and add in the fish stock.
5. Spoon all the remaining ingredients to the Instant Pot.
6. Close the lid and cook on a HIGH pressure for 30 minutes.
7. Release the pressure over 10 minutes.
8. Portion the soup into three bowls or mugs and dollop each bowl with the chopped parsley. Remember that this dish should be served warm.

Nutrition (Per Serving):

Calories: 215; Fat: 52g; Carbohydrates: 193g; Protein: 42g

Carp Heads Soup with Spanish Herbs

Serving: 4

Prep Time: 15 minutes

Cooking Time: 50 minutes

Ingredients:

- 5 carp heads
- 4 tablespoon sunflower oil
- 2 limes, cubed
- 2 teaspoons chili pepper powder
- 1 medium onion, thinly sliced
- 2 garlic cloves, smashed
- salt and pepper, to taste
- 1 cup of fish stock
- 5 cups of water
- ¼ cup of cilantro for garnish
- 1 teaspoon rosemary
- 1 teaspoon laurel (also called bay leaf)
- 1 teaspoon oregano
- 1 teaspoon basil
- 1 teaspoon thyme
- 1 teaspoon mint
- 1 bunch of parsley, chopped
- 1 bunch of dill, chopped

How to Prepare:

1. Set your Instant Pot to sauté mode and add some sunflower oil.
2. Add the chili pepper powder and sauté for 5 minutes.
3. Add the onion, 2 tablespoons cilantro, garlic and season with the salt and pepper.
4. Stir for 5 minutes and add the fish stock.
5. Season the carp heads with the salt and pepper and marinate for at least few hours unrefrigerated at room temperature.

6. In the Instant Pot, combine the ¼ cup of cilantro, 1 teaspoon rosemary, 1 teaspoon laurel (also called bay leaf), 1 teaspoon oregano, 1 teaspoon basil, 1 teaspoon thyme, 1 teaspoon mint, 1 bunch of parsley. Add the carp heads.

7. Mix all the remaining ingredients and close the lid and cook on a LOW pressure for 40 minutes.

8. Release the pressure over 10 minutes.

9. Portion the soup into four bowls or mugs and dollop each bowl with the chopped dill. Remember that this dish should be served warm.

<u>Nutrition (Per Serving):</u>

Calories: 251; Fat: 51g; Carbohydrates: 168g; Protein: 41g

Spicy Paleo Asian Soup

Serving: 5

Prep Time: 10 minutes

Cooking Time: 50 minutes

Ingredients:

- 40 oz salmon, diced
- 35 oz shrimps
- 10 oz Chinese noodles
- 1 cup of coconut milk
- 1 cup of lemon juice
- 3 cups of water
- 2 tablespoons olive oil
- ½ teaspoon salt and pepper
- 2 medium onions, chopped
- 1 teaspoon nutmeg
- 1 teaspoon chili powder
- 5 cloves minced garlic
- 1 bunch of greenery, chopped
- 1 tablespoon lemon juice

How to Prepare:

1. In a bowl, combine the nutmeg, chili, salt, garlic and black pepper. Season the shrimps with the spices mix. Set the shrimps aside to marinate for at least few hours unrefrigerated at room temperature or place in the fridge for overnight.
2. In the Instant Pot, heat the oil and sauté the shrimps for around 10 minutes until golden brown. Mix in the onions and stew for 10 minutes until clear and caramelized with the lid closed.
3. Combine the salmon, shrimps and all the remaining ingredients and add them to the Instant Pot. Pour some water.
4. Close the lid and cook on a MEDIUM pressure for 30 minutes.
5. Release the pressure naturally over 10 minutes.
6. Portion the shrimps into three bowls or mugs and dollop each bowl with the chopped greenery. Sprinkle some lemon juice. Serve the shrimps with the beer.

Nutrition (Per Serving)

Calories: 165; Fat: 26g; Carbohydrates: 59g; Protein: 25g

Paleo Spanish Fish Soup

Serving: 5

Prep Time: 15 minutes

Cooking Time: 60 minutes

Ingredients:

- 10 oz salmon
- 2 oz blanched almonds
- 1 medium onion, chopped
- 5 garlic cloves, smashed
- salt and pepper, to taste
- 1 cup of fish stock
- 1 teaspoon peppercorns
- 1 teaspoon saffron
- 1 teaspoon cumin
- 5 cups of water
- ¼ cup of cilantro
- 1 teaspoon rosemary
- 1 teaspoon basil

How to Prepare:

1. Season the salmon with the rosemary and salt and marinate for at least few hours unrefrigerated at room temperature.
2. In the Instant Pot, select the sauté mode and heat the oil. Sauté the almonds with the saffron, peppercorns, onions and garlic for 10 minutes until golden brown.
3. Add in the cilantro, basil and cumin and sauté for 5 minutes. Season with the salt and pepper.
4. Sauté for 5 minutes and add the fish stock.
5. Add the salmon and pour the water.
6. Close the lid and cook on a LOW pressure for 40 minutes.
7. Release the pressure over 10 minutes.
8. Portion the soup into five bowls or mugs and dollop each bowl with the basil. Remember that this dish should be served warm.

Nutrition (Per Serving):

Calories: 240; Fat: 47g; Carbohydrates: 160g; Protein: 37g

Paleo Fish Balls

Serving: 3

Prep Time: 10 minutes

Cooking Time: 30 minutes

Ingredients:

- 3 lb any fish, ground
- 2 tablespoons coconut oil
- 2 tablespoons garlic powder
- 2 tablespoons onion powder
- 1 tablespoon smoked paprika
- ¼ teaspoon each pepper and salt
- 1 bunch of greenery, chopped

How to Prepare:

1. Mix together garlic powder, onion powder, smoked paprika, salt and pepper.
2. Combine the ground fish with this mix.
3. Pour some coconut oil into the Instant Pot. Select the sauté mode and heat the oil in the Instant Pot.
4. Place the salmon balls into the Instant Pot. Close the lid and cook until brown on both sides. Cook on a MEDIUM pressure for 30 minutes.
5. Quick-release the pressure and open the lid.
6. Portion the fish balls into three plates or bowls and dollop each plate with the greenery. Serve the fish balls with the salad.

Nutrition (Per Serving):

Calories: 222; Fat: 31g; Carbohydrates: 173g; Protein: 31g

Fish with Almonds

Serving: 3

Prep Time: 5 minutes

Cook Time: 35 minutes

Ingredients:

- 3 halibut fillets
- 3 tablespoons white flour
- 2 eggs
- 1 cup of almonds, chopped
- 2 carrots, peeled and chopped
- 2 medium white onions, peeled and chopped
- 4 garlic cloves, chopped
- 4 tablespoons extra virgin olive oil
- 1 teaspoon turmeric
- ½ cup of water
- ½ a teaspoon cayenne pepper
- 2 teaspoons coriander
- 4 tablespoons lemon juice
- 2 tablespoons salt
- 1 tablespoon pepper

How to Prepare:

1. Preheat the oven to 250°-270°Fahrenheit and roast the chopped almonds in the oven for 10-15 minutes until lightly browned and crispy and then set aside.
2. In a bowl combine the minced garlic, with the turmeric salt and pepper. Toss the halibut fillets in this mix and sprinkle the lemon juice on top. Marinate the fish for at least 1 hour unrefrigerated.
3. In a bowl, whisk the eggs well. Spoon some salt and pepper and then mix well. Use the hand mixer.
4. Set the Instant Pot to the sauté mode and pour some extra virgin olive oil and heat it up. Spoon the onions and sauté for 5 minutes until clear and caramelized.

5. Mix in the carrots and simmer for 5 minutes until golden brown. Then spoon some salt and pepper. Mix in the coriander, cayenne pepper and turmeric. Mix well and close the lid for 10 minutes.
6. Meanwhile toss the halibut fillets in the eggs, flour and almonds.
7. Open the lid and place the halibut fillets inside the Instant Pot.
8. Pour some water and close the lid to cook on a MEDIUM pressure for 35 minutes. Release the pressure naturally and open the lid.
9. Portion the halibut fillets into three plates and sprinkle each plate with the pepper and lemon juice. Remember that this dish should be served warm. Serve the halibut fillets with the vegetables.

Nutrition (Per Serving):

Calories: 185; Fat: 35g; Carbohydrates: 116g; Protein: 32g

Conclusion

Thank you for buying this paleo instant pot cookbook. I hope this cookbook was able to help you to prepare fresh and healthy paleo instant pot recipes.

If you are new in this field of paleo instant pot cuisine, this book will help you to start your cooking journey. The recipes in this book are simple, and the process of cooking and preparing dishes is explained in the simple way. We also added some more complex recipes. Those you can cook, when you level of experience will grow and you will feel more confident. But never give up, always be open to learn and try something new!

Thank you again and I hope you have enjoyed this paleo cookbook.

Printed in Great Britain
by Amazon